A LIFE IN RHYME

By Bill Robertson

CCB Publishing
British Columbia, Canada

A Life in Rhyme

Copyright ©2014 by Bill Robertson
ISBN-13   978-1-77143-137-8
First Edition

Library and Archives Canada Cataloguing in Publication
Robertson, Bill, 1929-, author
A Life in Rhyme / by Bill Robertson. -- First edition.
Issued in print and electronic formats.
ISBN 978-1-77143-137-8 (pbk.).--ISBN 978-1-77143-138-5 (pdf)
Additional cataloguing data available from Library and Archives Canada

Front cover artwork provided courtesy of Alistair Reid: www.incallander.co.uk
The photo is of Glen Lyon (Scottish Gaelic: **Gleann Liomhann**) which is the ancestral home of the Robertson Clan. Located in Central Perthshire in Scotland, it is the longest enclosed glen in Scotland and runs for 34 miles from Loch Lyon in the west to the village of Fortingall in the east.

Back cover artwork depicts the Robertson Ancient Tartan and the Robertson Crest Badge, both of which are in the public domain and used herein without malice.

This work has been registered with the Canadian Intellectual Property Office:
Copyright Registration #1111859

Publisher: CCB Publishing
             British Columbia, Canada
             www.ccbpublishing.com

This book is dedicated to my wife, Sally, and my children;

Barbara, Christine, Marjory and Gregory.

Contents

Preface

The following is a collection of poetic or rhyming thoughts which I felt prompted, even inspired, to compose over the past sixty-two years and more. Most of them are rhyming, a few are blank verse, some are short and there is a scattering of Villanelles and Pantoums. All of them express a personal thought. I enjoy poetry as it can reach the heart of the matter in few words.

My mother's uncle David Gray* (1838-1861) was a published and nationally recognized poet in Scotland, while my paternal grandfather, William. B. Robertson wrote at least one descriptive rhyme.

At the Centenary Celebration of David Gray, in Edinburgh, there was a well-displayed exhibition of the poet's poems and many of his memorabilia. The host of the occasion, who was the Chairman of The Saltire Society asked me, as the poet's only living direct descendent, if I wrote any poetry. I said that I had written several small efforts. Immediately he responded that poetic talent was often passed on to a poet's succeeding generations and that I should certainly pursue my efforts which, I suppose, I have in a small way over the many years, as time and circumstance permitted. In his short life, David Gray pursued the writing of poetry as his one, consuming passion. For me it has largely been an intermittent urge.

In my eighty-fifth year, I decided to gather my poems together in one place, from various files, to satisfy my desire to have them close at hand as a reference in my remaining years. It is my hope that others may also find them of some interest.

Bill Robertson, March 2014

(*) **The Luggie and Other Poems** (1862) and, **Poetical Works** (1874) by David Gray

People and Places

No Resting Place *(1959)*

The winds blow cold and chill through the town, tis' winter
Tattered prayer flags flutter hopefully from the house tops
An evening sun imparts a golden brilliance to their faded glory
In the narrow street lamas, muliteers and tired, lonely women
Ebb and flow slowly, indecisive.

Where shall they go those exile wanderers from the past?
There is no resting place for them, only stops among strangers
On a road going down.

They came with questioning faces and sad hearts
Where shall we go? Is all their tragic mime
But one blessing theirs, they have no sense of time.

And we urgent minions of decaying foreign missions
Restless progeny of a Western church,
Striving, straining with outmoded tools, the Faith supreme
To spread
Our future too, does it not all uncertain lie ahead?

We too like them are strangers in a foreign land
Escapees from the turmoil of the 'wind of change'
Though they must go while we may stay,
Tis we are sad and happy they, if subtle truth be told,
Not they, but we at twilight stand, indecisive.

Poet's Comment: I wrote this poem one winter's evening as I sat on the verandah of Guild Mission House, looking over the town of Kalimpong in India.

It was 1959. Daily I was treating many Tibetan refugees in our hospital and clinics. They were those who had escaped the brutality of the Communist Chinese genocide of their country. They were supposedly the lucky ones. But as I thought about their situation, it was obvious that most of them could not remain in this small, mountain town. They had no resting place. The ironic similarity of their situation to that of Christian missionaries from the West struck me.

I had long realized that the second half of the twentieth century would be a time of monumental change. As a missionary, I realized that whether or not the hospital in Kalimpong would be taken over by Chinese troops or the Indian army, my future in Kalimpong was uncertain.

The great Western Christian Missionary enterprise of the 19th and 20th centuries in Asia was coming to an end. I was out of India in 1962 and most missionaries in India were gone by the 1980s.

Unfulfilled Dream *(1966)*

We stood on a shore of Time,
The sloping sand dry, warm, in the sun.
Your hand in mine, a life's love known
Too soon the coming of the tide.

Cold flows the water on the warm, dry sand
Yet cannot cool the spirit's bond.
In from the sea on some far off day
Quiet, in the ebb-tide, I'll open my eyes and find you waiting.

Crystal Cliffs *(1970)*

By the trefoil's sign there is warm sherry wine,
And the sound of the sea in my ears.
There are roses and posies and each day discloses
New light for the mind and fresh peace for the soul.

Our fair hostess attends us with sweet loving kindness
She's true like the heart of her land.
Where the crystal cliffs stand over warm sunlit sand
There is peace there in Antigonish.

Poet's Comment: Composed in April 1969 when an elderly lady on the north shore of Nova Scotia had invited several of us from Halifax, for a long week-end visit.

MacRobert's Disgrace *(1970)*

Twas in the year o'nineteen seventy
When chilly winds were blowin' a plenty.
MacRobert's min wi' greed wis bent
Tae tak the Rover, his intent.

Aince in a dream t'the ill-laid scheme
The Deil had quite converted him
And noo wi' April's end in view
His licence he must needs renew.

Sae noo tae Limond Ha' he sped
"A want yer cawr" he blithely said.
Sich sheer bare-faced affrontorie
The warld again may never see.

The ladies tried his plan 'dissuade
But twas nae guid, his min wis made.
Ane evenin' in the gloamin' mirk
He cam and at their hoose did lurk.

Ane hunner Holley'd gauged the fee
Wi' licence and new batterie
But Peter swore he'd trysted fifty
Guid sakes, wis e're the Deil mair thrifty.

An elder o' releegious bent
Ye'd thocht the angels he'd hiv kent
But oor heid man o' Treasurie
Wis ower fu o' humanitie.

Noo every day Lord Muck birls roon
The proodest man in auld Ayr toon.
Ye'd think the shame wid blin' his een
For a' ken he's the Deil's best frien!

Poet's Comment: In the decade before arriving in Canada I was friendly with Tom Limond and his sisters, Janie and Fay. Once I was in Canada, we corresponded and they told me in letters about how St. Leonard's Church and its members and how they were getting along. Mr. MacRobert was the Session Clerk and a man who liked the prominence of his position. The Limonds wrote about how he was determined to achieve a cheap second purchase of the Limonds 'expensive' Rover car. I composed the little poem in Scots to give it the authentic tone.

Riddell and the Hare *(1970)*

Bold Riddell's gone off to Barassie,
Run after a silver golf Tassie.
His departure will mean a re-group
In the ranks of the Ace Action Group.

St. Leonard's prime corps of religious
Is in depth and potential prodigious
So the loss of their leader so bold
Did not frighten or make their feet cold.

Nor did it enfrighten or scare
The noble long-legged March Hare.
Though with paws intertwined he did muse
And with rumbling and mumbling refuse.

When his head he put down tween his knees
It was really to ward off a sneeze.
If without such precaution he dares
He'd most certainly blow off his ears!

If because of such grievous neglect
He was cast from within the Elect
Such a folly so stupid and crass
Would have ruined his prize Bible class.

But when next at the Action Group meet
He was called to avert its defeat,
This most noble and excellent Hare
Accepted from the Group then, its Chair.

Poet's Comment: This was a whimsical comment on a Mr. Riddell, a worthy member of St. Leonard's Church on the news from the Limonds that he was planning to move to Barassie near the town of Troon, of golfing fame.

The Mad Meenister *(1971)*

Ane even' in spring, when the flooers bloomed sae sweet
The faithfu' few crept tae the peacefu' kirk meet.
In search o'contentment lik'coos tae thir feed
The Meenister's sermon they sat doon tae heid.

He ranted and raved aboot gourmets and gowfers
The evils o' picnics an' thirsty auld howfers.
And tae this they did hearkin' wi' self-righteous lugs
All noddin' thir heids lik' Pavlov's wee dugs.

An'syne as he blethered they noted a change
Some madness did threaten his min' tae derange.
"It isna' the weel but the waur ye should choose,
Come join me in praisin' the virtues o' booze!"

An auld buddy cried as she fainted an' fell
"If this is a' true, then am deid an' in Hell".
An' ithers were prayin they'd raither be deid,
The nicht that the Meenister went aff his heid!

Poet's Comment: Another wee poem in Scots about the time at an evening church service At St. Leonard's church when the minister the Rev. Campbell Saunders preached a sermon against the current evils in the society of the town of Ayr. However the Limonds reported that halfway through his message he appeared to lose his train of thought and encourage these evil ways!

Dreich Dug Ditty *(1972)*
(Or Melancholy Musings before a Dog Show).

Ah've a pug, wha' a mug,
Furtae gie ma wee black dug!
Whit a shame maks ye lame,
Just tae see its wee bit wame.
Auntie Jean seen the Queen
Stottin'doon St. James's green
Thocht she hid a pug-lik dogy
But it wis a Welsher's corgie.

Still ah'll go tae the Show,
Pit a ribbon roun its toes
Ony judge if he's wise
'll gie ma dug the Booby Prize.

Pean Pense *(1972)*

Auntie Jean's no been seen
Since she sat apone a pean.
Maybe she's got fair absorbi'
Birlin'roun an' roun in orbi'!

Poet's Comment: Two little whimsical thoughts in a Glasgow dialect. If translations are necessary talk to a Glaswegian of your acquaintance.

St. Leonard's Loup *(1972)*

The kirk it held its Social Nicht
An' gied auld Ayr an awfi' fricht!
In Bellisle Ha' they did assemble
An soon the wa's began tae tremble.

The guests sat roun an' ate fu' hearty
Then leered and laich'd at stories dirty!
An' syne as ye'll nae doot jaloose
They soon were stappit up wi' booze!

Then neist at Tammy Timlett's ca'
They rose as wan tae stert the Ba'
In loupin', screechin, houlin craze
They a' began tae daff thir claes!
An' on an' on wi' sich-lik levity
They slippet doun tae foul depravity!
The Meenister sare he rant an' raved
An' mercy fur them a' he craved.

Auld Nick himsel' tis said wis there
He'd cam tae teach, but stayed tae stare!
Said he, "Whit maks me really happy
Tis a congregation fu' o' nappy!"

But efter tae the Guid Ca' hearkinin'
The Meenister gart a fearfu'reckonin'!
He set them a' tae tearfu' thinkin'
Anent the sins o' social drinkin'!

Poet's Comment: Another little offering in Scots about a somewhat exaggerated but hopefully amusing account of the annual Kirk Social held at Bellisle Hall near Ayr. In 2003, I gave a copy of it to "The Meenister", Rev. Campbell Saunders. He liked it.

Campbell Capers *(1974)*

Campbell Saunders gave a roar
When he saw the lights galore.
"Whit," said he, "is a' this waste?
Extinguish a', be dark encased!"

But as they sat in pews quite darkly
His flock engaged in high malarkey!
Too late he realized his folly
And first did utter only, "Golly".

To darkness foul he'd them consigned
"Oh cruel Fate twas Thee designed,
This cunning plot and me ensnared,
A' cannie even see ma beard!"

"Oh Beadle please restore the licht
An' gie us back the power o' sicht.
A'll ne'er again be rash an' Shout
Tae hae' the blessed licht put out."

And soon they sat in brightness bathed
A host of Ayrshire sinners saved,
From what I'll make no recitation
But leave to your imagination!

Poet's Comment: Another response to a letter the Limonds sent commenting on a church lighting problem, one Sabbath evening service.

Mrs. Duster *(1975)*

Every evening by the clock
Without warning, sign or knock,
Purposeful within her bounds
Mrs.Duster does her rounds.

With firm resolve and measured tread,
She strides the house from bed to bed.
Some deep felt urge herself she grants
In seeking out each pair of pants.

The garment once within her sight
She grasps it strong with all her might
And thrusting through the open pane
She makes it clean with might and main.

Such seeming ritual acts indeed
Excite an anthropological heed.
In pondering such a thing so queer
We yet might life's confusion clear.

A host of possibilities
Do stimulate our expertise
A fetish might the answer be
For such a trouser-trailing spree.

Again, it may be just that zeal
Which all good nurses 'ere do feel
In keeping certain clothing free
Of every bed-bug, louse or flea.

A trait of strong inheritance
Might compel this nightly dance.
Imbued with sturdy farm-wife's will
Her grandmamma she follows still.

Though science and philosophy
May oft confuse both you and me
We'll 'ere enjoy that night-show yonder
And stand and gaze in awe and wonder.

Poet's Comment: One summer evening when I was weeding the front garden of our house in Ottawa, my curiosity was aroused by what I thought was the rather odd behavior of the lady in the house on the other side of the street. A brief observation of her actions highlighted by the evening sun, revealed a somewhat strange, but in its way amusing ritual, which I took notice of on at least one other evening later that month. The lady who I learned had a number of young children, mainly boys, had been a nurse and was a fanatic for cleanliness. She did a nightly round of the upstairs bedrooms, flinging open each window, then vigorously shaking pairs of pants and jeans in the open air. This repeated spectacle inspired my imagination to concoct this offering.

Ella McGlynn - ("Oh come on!" Ella) *(1977)*

Mrs. Ella McGlynn is as proud of her kin,
As the rest of the Edinburgh Clan.
This Merchiston maid puts all else in the shade,
She could never say "cant" only "can"!

Whatever the challenge she answers the call,
She doesn't say maybe, it's nothing or all.
If you think you are busy, let Ella arrive,
And soon you'll be looking more dead than alive!

Of wit and good nature she's full to the brim,
Her Gillespies' true colours will never grow dim.
A fine lady of whom it will always be said,
She's hard-working, kindly, loyal and well-bred!

I've worked here and there in the East and the West,
With some of the worst and a few of the best,
But whatever the past or the future may bring,
I'll be proud to have known Mrs. Ella McGlynn!

Poet's Comment: Ella McGlynn was my secretary during several of the years I worked in the Canadian Federal Department of Health and Welfare as Director. It was a busy job and full of the challenges from issues from across the ten provinces of Canada and locally from the insidious take-over of Canada's government in the interests of Quebec. Ella was an immigrant Scot like me, older than me and as I later discovered, a severe diabetic. She was an inspiration to work with. Unfortunately she passed away some years later.

Kingston General *(1977)*

In Kingston town there lives a chiel
And everyone, they love him weel.
A worthy man whom all respect,
A friend of mine is James.B.Flett.

Where stood our national Parliament
He stands alone on duty bent.
With knowledge, power and much to give,
He is the top executive.

A member of the C.H.A.,
He's served it well for many a day.
Elected to its chief Committee,
A man of wisdom, bright and witty.

At home he's found in married bliss,
With children, dog and Moira's kiss.
Surrounded thus with joys replete,
He stands, a man, secure, complete.

Poet's Comment: I wrote this for Jim after I met him over 30 years after he had been in my class at school at Allan Glen's. He was the Administrator of the Kingston General Hospital and later became the Chief Executive Officer at the biggest hospital in Vancouver.

Dr. Derek Gellman *(1978)*

Among those who came over from Old England dear,
There are hundreds and thousands we laud and revere.
But of all of that clan, Derek Gellman's our man,
Who has built up a brilliant, outstanding career.

He had many a ploy in old Illinois,
With renal filtration 'twas no mere flirtation,
And many's the kidney of sober or tiddly,
He rid of disease, obnoxious and piddly.

When one day he heard tell to the north was a land,
Which because of the weather, there was great demand,
For nephrologist's skills to cure renal ills;
Something very much more than just bed rest and pills.

With provinces stretching to east and to west,
He thought in the middle would really be best.
So donning some long drawers, a parka and more,
He took all his knowledge near Assiniboine's shore.

Soon concerned by the high cost of nephrology,
To Winnipeg's socialist economy,
He worked with great grit on cost benefit,
To see if it could be improved a bit.

In monograms lucid and elegant,
He tutored the federal elephant.
Impressed by the wit of this erudite Brit.,
It lured him to Ottawa's top elite.

Established in Ottawa's bilingual crew,
He soon understood how to say "parlez-vous".
'Mong Newfies, Blue Nosers and Quebecois too,
With folks from the West and Torontonians blue.

There were times he had trouble in being understood
And in making his point as a bureaucrat should.
He mused and reflected on how that could be
Since the only one speaking "sans accent" was he.

But once involved in top Federal planning
And of all the problems of health system manning,
It did not take too long for him to catch on,
To the need broad and deep to establish a Norme.

As he hoisted the ensign of standards,
The "Watch-Docs" all reached for their lanyards.
Their senses aghast, they gave out a blast
"Gainst the threat which this posed to their privileged caste.

But our hero so noble, so bold and so true,
Said we'll standardize cervical ca screening for you,
And with consummate ease, sailed in on a breeze,
With a study that made the national news.

But wise men flew in one day from the West,
Determined to look out for only the best.
Leaving no stone unturned, lest their bid become spurned,
They offered a gown and the Vice-President's crown.

So soon he'll be off to be most on the coast,
Over empires he'll rule, if not always boast.
His Queen by his side in a castle reside
With magnificent views to be seen far and wide.

Now in making your journey out to the West,
Be sure that you fly in Air Canada's best,
'Cause we're all quite concerned as to whether you can,
If you drive o'er the Rockies in your old blue sedan.

Here's the best of good luck to you both as you go,
And we want you and Vera to always know,
That we think as top brass, you're truly first class
And we wish very much you did not have to go.

So may happiness, joy and good fortune be yours,
And every success and renown your rewards,
We all wish you the best and we say as your friend,
Remember, come back here and see us again.

Poet's Comment: Composed on the occasion of Dr. Derek Gellman's farewell party, September 1978. Derek was an Englishman and an immigrant. To be sung, if necessary, to the tune of "Vive l'Amour".

Laura Desjardins *(1980)*

A certain lady we all know,
Our Admin work, she made it go.
The Queen of Hearts, she ran the show,
But now she's going and it's a blow.

With budget blues and work-plan woes,
You helped us vanquish all such foes;
And also kept us on our toes!
We'll miss you Laura, heaven knows.

When claims came in defying description,
Enough to give a man "Kniptions"!
You soon could part the facts from fiction,
and saved us all much sore affliction.

Reports on leave or variance,
Which we might overlook perchance,
Or even eye with view askance,
You led us ably through the dance.

In M.R.O.s dark jungle deep,
Where P.S Travel demons creep,
And O.B.S. and E.D. Peep,
You saved us from the final leap.

Organogrammes and contracts too,
Or publications gone askew,
These put us often in a stew,
But all were simple things to you.

In conference work you were supreme,
You organized and led the team,
Unanimous we all do deem,
In this you were and are the Cream.

Perhaps 'tis here I should just mention,
There were odd moments of some tension,
As when at one august convention,
You caused some little apprehension.

When rushing in someone to seek;
We know you were not there to peep!
But still a blush did grace your cheek,
On finding him about to leak!

If all your deeds we did recite,
We'd take at least another night,
Of parties, presents, cards, we'd cite,
and how you make rum cake, just right.

So Laura dear, we want to say,
How we've admired you every day,
We'll not forget you, come what may,
We'd love it if you just would stay.

Poet's Comment: Composed on the occasion of Laura's retirement party at Le Cercle Universitaire, Ottawa. Laura was always an Anglophone, despite her French name. Many of us were leaving the Federal government in Ottawa at that time, a story which one day will be told.

The Scotty Lambs *(1989)*

I send you a toast,
From the far eastern coast,
So please doff your tams,
To the two Scotty Lambs.

As the Hospital's king,
He's had a full fling,
And made them all sing,
To his Yang and his Ying.

After years as the honcho,
He's put on a wee poncho,
But never you mind,
He's the best of his kind.

And good wishes too,
I send Mrs. Ewe,
For keeping her Ram,
Both spritely and calm.

As you feast on prime ribs,
Here's a toast to their nibs,
"May your lum reek lang
O'er a guid lang whang!"

Poet's Comment: A colleague asked me to compose something for the retirement party of their old colleague out West in Calgary, Dr. Scott Lamb. I had never met the man, but apparently he liked it. He was a Scot.

Sir Martin Boyd of Torphichen *(1990)*

Sir Martin Boyd of Torphichen
Was sired in '23,
At Stirling High he made his mark
An Esquire noble, he.

To auld St. Andrew's cloister then
This 'prentice knight did go
And working long with might and main
His spurs he soon did show.

Once mounted on his medic's steed
He rode to serve his Queen
Was soon reviewing sick parades
Of soldiers, fat and lean.

Returning then to "Civvy Street"
He galloped to Dundee
A noble Doc whom all could meet
Ane kilted Scotch G.P.

Ah then did Cupid's happy barb
Reveal to him his queen
And striding forth in festive garb
He claimed his fair Irene.

But hark! The trumpet call I hear
Fetch me my sword and spear,
To Canada! To Canada!
For duty and career.

And thus so many years ago
The knight and lady both
Arrived in fair Saskatchewan
And took the Prairie Oath.

A family practitioner
He settled down to be
The Swift Current folks enjoying his burr
Soon trusted none but he.

For some long years he did prescribe
To heal the sick and suffering
Then turned upon a brilliant vibe
To medical administering.

A bureaucrat he thus became
Exchanging 'scope for quill
And checking each practitioner's claim
Controlled the final bill.

The years in quick succession passed
In many lists he fought
The quill-like spear was wearing fast
Twas time to change his lot.

And so to Winnipeg he came
Just after '79
With DVA to make his name
As RMO full fine.

Soon, soon he did them organize
In treatment plans exact
Each detailed clause both apt and wise
He honed with sense and tact.

At many long RMOC's
He was of great renown
The chairman loved his "Time out, please"
Which kept incont'nence down.

The list is long the stories true
Of noble things he did
But one at least I think is due
Of which I do not kid.

Of great respectability
He'd never ere offend,
At Cleopatra's table he
One night his eye did bend.

The scene was set, the air was tense
With Oriental thrall
Sir Martin rose to leap the fence
To heed his knightly call.

Allah Ackbar! Cried every codger
The drums throbbed for the dance
T'was Scotland's world champ, Tummy Twitcher
Oh what a lecherous prance!

But scarce the victory had been won
Our knight in joy he sings
"Oh now I know what should be done
I'll change my spurs for wings!

And soon this nouveau chevalier
Was soaring high in air so clear
Above the clouds of TAPS and VIP
Enjoying an acrobatic flip.

Across the Manitoba sky
He customarily will fly
Returning soon to well-loved scene
Sir Martin and Irene.

In future years we'll see them still
These trusty friends our hearts will fill
And on this day we join to say
God bless you both upon your way.

Poet's Comment: This is a poem/ballad composed for one of my medical staff on the occasion of his retirement. Like the others I recited it at his retirement party. I think he liked it, but he didn't say.

Thank you *(1991)*

My thanks to every one of you
For kindly thoughts and wishes true.
With rehabilitative care
I'm slowly reaching full repair.

Poet's Comment: A note to my staff in the office in Charlottetown when I, for a rare time, I was off having hernial repair surgery.

Leaving *(1992)*

Waiting to leave; my desk is cleared
Of all but impersonal gadgets of my trade.
The blotting pad and telephone, a Dictaphone
And shiny varnished wooden trays, both "In" and "Out".

Scotch tape in its orange dispenser and three-hole
Punch, a swingline stapler, paper clips glistening
In their twin grooved solid glass dish.

The desk and drawers undressed of many work-a-day
knick-knacks, reveals proud oak polished in warm
brown hued tones of solid richness which has
served me faithfully ten years now.

An empty feeling in my gut
A sudden poignance that I'm going for good
Unlamented and forgot, save by this mute brown wood.

The clock buzzer sounds, its time to go
The clashing noise and fuss of my next-door neighbour
As he tries to survive, dashes all sentiment into brittle shreds,
dissolving doubts and speeding my retreating steps. I'm gone.

Poet's Comment: A short poem to myself on the day I retired from the Department of Veterans Affairs. Gone with no fuss.

Cobbled Cookies at St. John's *(2007)*

No cookies today, we have to say,
From now on that must be the way.
If with your coffee or cup of tea
A tasty cookie you'd like to see.

Although 'tis true you're old and gray,
And view this change with much dismay,
Remember in this modern age
The elderly are off the stage.

But if by end of Service time
The thought of cookies is sublime,
Be sure to bring your own supply
And end the morn upon a high.

Pantoum on Door County Days *(2009)*

We'll always remember Door County days
First up the west past Old Stone Quarry Park
The harbors and islands, the ports and the bays
With beauty and charm they all made their mark.

First up the west past Old Stone Quarry Park
By Horseshoe Road to Egg Harbor Bay
With beauty and charm they all made their mark
And on to Fish Creek looking out on Green Bay.

By Horseshoe Road to Egg Harbor Bay
Then Ephraim's old Nordic Moravian mood
After passing Fish Creek looking out on Green Bay
Then a Sister Bay lunch of fine Swedish food.

Then Ephraim's old Nordic Moravian mood
Through Ellison Bay and on to Gills Rock
Having dined on a lunch of fine Swedish food
It was time to turn round as we looked at the clock.

Through Ellison Bay and on to Gills Rock
Then by Bailey's Harbor and Kangaroo Lake
It was time to move on as we looked at the clock
Through Jackson Port, Valmy, was the route we did take.

Our journey over our hearts had an ache
We'll always remember Door County days
Our memories there we shall never forsake
The harbors and islands, the ports and the bays.

Poet's Comment: Door County, Wisconsin is indeed pleasant.

Villanelle on Louise *(2009)*

If you should need transcription, ask Louise
It doesn't matter if it's short or long
With artful skill she'll find the piece with ease.

I tried myself to write the doh-re-mees
But all my efforts always came out wrong
If you should need transcription ask Louise.

A composition full of different keys
I could have searched from Moscow to Hong Kong
With artful skill she'll find the piece with ease.

Concertos, fugues from Bach to Viennese
For sure it's not like ludo or ping-pong
If you should need transcription ask Louise.

So when you're almost desperate, do please
Remember to seek the help of Madam Deschamps
With artful skill she'll find the piece with ease.

And so I recommend that all should seize
The opportunity to catch your song
If you should need transcription ask Louise
With artful skill she'll find the piece with ease.

Poet's Comment: In my violin scrapings I sought new and inexpensive music to play. It proved a difficult search until I happened upon Louise Deschamps who told me the key to finding inexpensive sheet music. She disappeared before I could give her this little thanks.

Pantoum on Neighbours *(2009)*

The neighbours round our garden are happy and sedate
As quietly in comfort they read the daily news
They know they also serve who only sit and wait
While forming their opinions on all the varied views.

As quietly in comfort they read the daily news
They understand too clearly their days are passing fast
While forming their opinions on all the varied views
They realize with wisdom their time will soon be past.

They understand too clearly their days are passing fast
While still to sundry faults and foibles they do cling
They realize with wisdom their time will soon be past
Although from time to time they long for one last fling.

While still to sundry faults and foibles they do cling
A senior generation is worthy of respect
Although from time to time they long for one last fling
Still hoping to be counted among their God's elect.

A senior generation is worthy of respect
The neighbours round our garden are happy and sedate
Still hoping to be counted among their God's elect
They know they also serve who only sit and wait.

Retirement Home Ladies *(2011)*

She looked at me with hesitation,
When I mentioned reincarnation,
I'd seen and heard her once before,
In far off place that was no more.
We talked of family and of friends
And wonder what it all intends.

The other ladies much the same,
Had lived their lives devoid of fame.
They concentrated on sons and daughters,
While men they thought were mainly rotters.
I'm sure they'd all been clean and pure,
Though one I thought but wasn't sure.

Now most of them are on their own,
Sitting out their time alone.
Too soon 'tis time to end their stay,
And take their spirits far away.

She walks with sticks most every day,
Determined still to wend her way.
To hold out for another season,
Her daughter is her only reason.

Lily and Rosie the queens of Mah Jongg
They know when its time to say 'Pong',
And sometimes it's a 'Chee' they see,
That leads to Mah Jongg victory.

Some others long past four and twenty,
Are sharp and quick with brains aplenty,
But need to use a walking aid,
As hips and knees begin to fade.

At evening Bridge they're always witty,
Tho' when they lose it is not pretty.
At Bingo they can all excel,
And joy to give a winning yell.

There's some who love the Carpet Bowls,
Which captivates these friendly souls,
The latest craze to play is Wii,
For which they'll have to form a queue.

And some there are who're racked with pain
With every bend and twist and strain
They've had their hips and knees replaced
Which some might say they did in haste,
And better could have exercised
Their joints to be happy, if surprised.

Poet's Comment: An early thought that still stands of a Retirement Home.

Retirement Home Men *(2011)*

The men of Berwick are an admirable crew
As one of them I can vouch 'tis true.
While arrogance is a common trait
These macho males enjoy their fate.
In life we've adopted a way that's fitter
Maybe it helped to be top of the litter.
Having said all that with an air of certainty
I must admit we're not priority.
As the years have passed we've all realized
It's not as once we had surmised
As Kings we do not rule serene
For each of us our wife is Queen.

Some have traveled far and wide
Others await the silent tide.
All have stories to relate
Of things they love, a few they hate.
But mostly it's of family
Things they did when twenty three.
Or how their daughters' hearts were won
Their sons' careers and what they've done.
There's some that see their lives as small
While others feel they've done it all.
Some are younger some are old
But all their tales are solid gold.

There's this guy that's suave and tall
Who knows for sure he's seen it all.
Yet as he sips his evening tea
He learns he may have more to see
Of aging problems still to come
From which he likely will succumb.

Many here don't hear so well
What others say they just can't tell.
But with a grin they do their best
To understand and keep abreast
Of every thought and word and clue
That comes along for their review.

Poet's Comment: Berwick Men: The men seem somewhat fitter than men of their age in the general community. Most Canadian men have died before reaching 80. While the majority of Berwick men are over 80 some also in their 90s and several over 100. Thus being fitter and stronger, Berwick men have survived longer than those in the general community. Nevertheless they have more illness than the women. For much of their lives I would estimate they had dominated their wives, but most now seem to be dominated by their wives. Presumably, their aggression and testosterone have lessened with age and this is likely a major factor in their longevity.

Berwick Meals *(2011)*

Breakfast

The oldest residents always come first
Maybe its hunger, maybe its thirst.
They tuck in to cereal, bacon and egg,
With coffee and tea, they don't have to beg.
There's seconds and fill-ups whatever they want
It's certain they're ready to leave on a jaunt.

Then come the eight o'clock, eight-thirty and nines,
Discussing their stocks and looking for signs.
But more than all these the Diners and Dash
Who want to get on with their lives in a splash.
Whatever the time they all feel sublime
Each is quite ready to get out for a climb.

Mid-Morning and Mid-Afternoon Bistros

Mid-morning and mid-afternoon,
Bistro-time can't come too soon.
It's time to have a cup of tea,
And chat with friends we like to see.

A muffin or a cookie sweet,
We all enjoy this little treat.
Exchange the latest news and views,
Of health or sickness, trips or cruise.
A welcome pause, a time to share,
A time to feel, a time to care.

Some doctors teach not to eat between meals
While others say, a little and often.
At the Berwick Royal Oak such advice is a joke,
As we eat when we like and its heaven.

Lunch

Soup or juice, entrée or sandwich
Salad and veggies we love them all.
A little dessert or a cup of tea
And time for a chat, it's the best it can be.

Dinner

Dinner times here are from five to six-thirty,
It's a time to dress up and look wise or just flirty.
People are chatty and talk of the past,
When the times were good and still not too fast.
One lady remembers all the children she had,
Most were good all the time, only one not too bad.

Poet's Comment: I enjoy all the meals, except that I don't eat at the Bistro times, otherwise I would be eating five times a day!

Berwick Outlooks *(2011)*

An old man looks out to the highway
He counts the traffic on the Pat Bay.
Every minute hundreds pass
Hurtling ever, cars en masse.
This way that way never ending
Some ascending some descending.

Hundreds passing by the hour
Guided missiles fired by power.
Now and then the siren's wail
Police cars on a speedster's tail.
And sometimes its two Fire trucks speeding
To fire or crash they're oft proceeding.
And some fly past when more than late
Some guy returning from a date.

Berwick Royal Oak *(2011)*

Berwick Royal Oak is a model retirement home,
Of that there is not a shadow of doubt.
Now that we're here there's no need to roam,
Happy, contented we don't want to get out.

On arrival we met with efficient Reception,
Helen Brown's welcome is friendly and warm,
We knew we were centres of caring attention,
Surrounded by love, protected from harm.

Our suite is exactly the size that we needed,
Large windows, fine drapes, good bathrooms and heating,
The standard of fittings could not be exceeded,
The parking is handy, adjoining our wing.

Where else in the world are such varied activities,
Wonderful staff and range of amenities?

The Noise-Mungers *(2012)*

The Noise-mungers upstairs are at it again
We don't know why and we never know when.

Today it sounded like carpet laying,
Using nails hammered right into the boards.
It was during our time for meditation and praying,
We didn't feel drawn to offer rewards.

The male is a European the female is a Brit,
He does carpentry, she moves crates.
When he saws wood, she shakes out bedding,
If its not a divorce it cant be a wedding!

Then suddenly they moved away,
Where they went no one can say.
A stranger two we've never met,
What they want we hope they'll get.

Sonnet for Bruce *(2012)*

Bruce was a man of courage,
Faced the world as straight and true
Someone at a ripe old age
Whose message was not old, but new.

Someone that I scarcely met
At breakfasts where we sat and ate
Our wives enjoyed a chat and let
Us solve life's problems and our fate.

A family filled with generations
Four fine daughters and their children
Fulfilling all their aspirations
Only asking where or when.

He lay in someone else's site,
His grandsons fought and put it right.

Sonnet to a Lady *(2012)*

A lady who does understand
That judgment must be always fair.
She walks her way in full command
And still presents a regal air.
Long years reflect her ready wit,
Oft warmed with humor's kindly gift
Developed as life's way saw fit,
Rewarding all with timely lift.
With wisdom she is ever blest,
As honest as the day is long.
One trusts her word, it is the best.
Its always right and never wrong.

In life one needs both strength and courage,
And she has both to last an age.

Tin Man II *(2013)*

As I look out upon the garden
My Tin Man thoughts do slowly harden,
On why the Denfords placed it there,
Was I supposed to stand and stare?

At first I felt they could have asked us
But that would just have caused a fuss.
Perhaps they had a random thought,
It was a Tin Man that they bought.

After the Tin Man was in Oz,
He was very happy because,
As Emperor of Winkie Land,
His subjects answered his command.

At Berwick as we lie asleep,
The Tin Man's light a watch does keep.
So we can all be safe and sound
Enjoying the haven we have found.

Berwick Pets *(2013)*

Pets are now allowed at Berwick
Dogs and cats, you take your pick.
We'd prefer a German Shepherd
Though some might choose a friendly leopard.

Some may think that sounds quite mad
But future years may make us sad,
As younger folk expand their friendships
To beasts that come from wilder fellowships.

A lady may befriend a doe
An old man may prefer a crow.
Some could have a different style
And introduce something quite vile.

Rats and mice, lizards and snakes,
Enough to give one a dose of the shakes!
Crocodiles and alligators looking for a bite
Waddling round the dining room, would give one quite a fright!

Budgies, parrots, frisky antelopes,
Fulfilling resident's dreams and hopes.
Head Office nightmares will transpire,
At least one CEO will retire.

Who Lifted My Laundry? *(2014)*

One day an old lady 'lifted' my laundry
And left me confused and deep in a quandary.
Why would she do this, I asked myself squarely
It seemed so obvious she was acting quite queerly.

From where in the world had this odd-ball appeared?
Was it Oak Bay or Saanich, some place much revered?
Or far out in the boonies where we don't want to go
Perish the thought if it turned out to be true!

I'm not really snobbish but what would you do?
If your togs had been handled by a hag with the flu.
It's a problem for sure, but I think without doubt
That I'd have in the end just to throw them all out.

Family and Friends

Bill Robertson

Kalimpong *(1959)*

It was totally unexpected, but surely I should have known.
Walking quietly down the compound hill
A day's work done, but never really over,
In the motley collection of aging buildings
Dignified by the name of "hospital".

Autumn leaves were gently falling as I passed the church
The familiar, well-worn path welcoming me home,
Sweeping round the corner, the beauty of the Teesta valley
Always made me momentarily pause, breathing in its refreshment.
Up the verandah steps, through the open door
The sound of my footsteps on the polished wooden floor
Contrasting with an eerie silence.
No babies' cry or gurgle, no friendly creaking of a mother's step upstairs
Only utter silence!

Quickly sensing something different, through
to the dining room and on to the kitchen at the back.
A kindly, quiet, steady look on Pratap's face,
His laconic, "Memsahib gayo, Nanihuroo gayo!"

They're gone, where to, when, why, the questions
shrieking in my head, but only the brief queries answered,
"This morning, just after you left for the hospital
in a garry, all four left, going with much luggage,
to Siliguri, maybe Calcutta ? Who Knows?"

Supper alone, silent except for the little clattering of dishes
and cutlery and the sound of my own chewing, loud in my ears.
"More bhat sahib?" "No dhanyabad, not hungry."
Why the screaming in my head, the dizziness?
A thousands reasons milling around, a rare pain in the back of my head,
What does it mean? … Life will never be the same again.

Poet's Comment: In 1959, I had been a Presbyterian medical missionary working in India for four years. Communist China had committed the genocide of Tibet and thousands of their troops were then on the threshold of India, poised, it was said, to invade and conquer India.

At the time, the hospital at which I worked was only a short drive from the border of Tibet, but my duty was treating the sick and I intended to stay and continue to perform my duty. My wife (first) had a different view. Since arriving in India I had come to realize that she was not happy as a missionary. That evening as I tried to grasp what she had done, it dawned on me that with three small children the likelihood of the arrival of Chinese troops was too much, so she had left without discussion. Whatever her reasons it came as a great shock to me.

Incidentally, the Chinese troops did not arrive and still have not over fifty years later.

To Barbara *(1961)*

A Happy Birthday, Barbara
On this your special day.
Fond love and kisses Daddy
Sends to you from far away.

Its February second
God bless this happy morn,
Our thanks to Him we offer
On this day when you were born.

This is your day of honor
Our charming dark-eyed maid,
And so with presents large and small
Our fond respects we've paid.

All thanks then to our Father
Who shared this mortal life
And give to Him, who gave His Son
At least, your all, your life.

Poet's Comment: This was composed for Barbara's second birthday when I was still in Kalimpong, India.

Barbara *(1961)*

Thy great renown, Oh! Bunny Brown,
I'll shout afar from town to town.
No other man by land and sea
A daughter has to equal thee.

Marjory *(1961)*

Where the ships go Whoo! Whoo!
When the tide's flowing high
And the fire engine's siren is rushing on by
And people and places too many to tell
Till you're falling asleep in your own little shell.
With a paw full of muzz
Near a warm little snout
And I'll be so happy I'll jump up and shout.

Its not very long now
I'm counting the days
Till I see you again
And your nice little ways.
We'll all hug together then
Snug in our flat
And what could be better, I ask you, than that?

Christine *(1961)*

Oh! Badger! Oh! Badger! I'm longing to see
Your stripy sweet self sitting up on my knee.
Your fur is so soft and so furry and warm
Your smile full of beauty, your eyes full of charm.

Poet's Comment: Sent in a letter to my daughters Barbara, Marjory, and Christine when the family was in Scotland and I was still in Kalimpong, India.

Christine and Marjory's Bedtime Song *(1962)*

Christine and Marjory are going to bed
Two little girls with very sleepy heads.
That Dreamland chu-chu train is calling
And soon you'll both asleep be falling.

Christine and Marjory are saying a prayer
"Thank you Lord Jesus for all your love and care.
Forgive us for the times we've not been good
And help us do just what we should".

Christine and Marjory are fast asleep
O'er their little beds Jesus watch will keep.
He loves them both so tenderly
And they'll be safe the whole night through.

Poet's Comment: I composed this little ditty after I got home to Scotland. I sang it to the twins, Christine and Marjory, to the accompaniment of my guitar when they were tucked up in bed. They often fell asleep before it was finished.

Barbara's Bed-Time Song *(1962)*

Sleepy, sleepy, Barbara
Now its time for bed
Time to go to Dreamland
And be snug in bed.

Sleepy, sleepy, Barbara
Time to say a prayer,
Time to thank Lord Jesus
For all His love and care.

We give thanks Lord Jesus
For all happiness
We are little children
And Thy Name we bless.

Sleepy, sleepy, Barbara
Jesus safe will keep
Through the night till morning
While she lies asleep.

Poet's Comment: This was also sung to a little tune which I composed along with the ditty and accompanied on my guitar. Like the twins she usually fell asleep before I finished.

Bye-gone Days *(1969)*

Busy the life for all but the rich in the bye-gone days of King Eddy,
When the girls were gay on a summer's day and the trombone went tarara-reddy.
What a joy to be on the Eagle III, when the German bands were playing,
See the paddles whirl and the waters swirl, hear the boys and the sailors a'hailing.

But now too soon we're off to the Moon in fine flashing space-ships a'sailing,
Where we'll try to forget with no sigh of regret that virtue is gone unavailing.
And fixedly gaze into limitless space where we're sure we will meet the Eternal
And who knows recapture the joys and the rapture of idyllic Edwardian sailing.

Poet's Comment: Sent to my mother back in Scotland in June 1969 as a thought about when she
had been a young girl in the carefree time in Britain in the years before WW I.

To My Daughters *(1980)*

I want you to know
You'll always be dear to me.
What's always been true,
How special you are to me.

How I was the first human being
in this world to see you.
How you are uniquely a part of me,
And carry that part on into the future.

You are special to yourselves,
God's unique creation,
Like no other, to be cherished
as sacred creatures.

You are given by God,
To embody your everlasting souls
On this planet, as something that never was before
And never will be the same as you again.

You are special to God.
He has watched over you
since you were conceived,
And He will receive your soul,
at your life's end.

I want you to know that I'm thankful
for the gift that your lives mean.
Thankful for the opportunity
God has given us to live on this Earth
as sacred, sanctified beings.

Poet's Comment: Written four years after my marriage to Sally Linkert and when the girls had gone off on their own.

To A Daughter *(1980)*

Communicate ! communicate!
If you think that you'll be late.
One word only said in time,
Makes relationships sublime.

Poet's Comment: This was composed after one of my daughters had left home to study at university in Toronto.

Thoughts of Mother *(1980)*

I recall:
And I remember childhood days,
When you did guard my every step,
That nothing bad would me befall
And all I had to do was call.

And soon you came, by night or day
And listened then to what I'd say,
Some comfort find to smooth my way,
Yes, I recall.

Mither:
And see her wee bit figure
Hirplin'oot o'sicht tae board the plane,
And fly the cold wide ocean all alain,
Undaunted yet.

O mither dear how I wid feign
Catch sicht o' you aince mair,
As aince we met.

Poet's Comment: This was composed a year after mother passed away. Although nobody in our immediate family had spoken in Scots in several generations I felt moved to write the second part in that tongue. Maybe something out of mother's weaving family background at Merkland motivated me.

Dad Ditty *(1986)*

Mrs. Marjory Phillips of Grand Forks BC,
Has clearly established her identity.
A lady at home sheeting sail or on ski,
And expert in medical technology.

A year has gone by since the wedding took place,
Twas a red-letter day for Marjory Grace.
The youngest of three all in satin and lace,
She's now with James William setting the pace!

In life it's ideal to be sure of your goals,
And work to complete ones body and soul.
There are times to go slow or you land in a hole,
I've seen it myself and it sure takes its toll!

Success in this life is to know who you are,
And strive after balance as you reach for your star.
Mrs. Marjory Phillips of Grand Forks you are,
Wife to your David and daughter to Pa!

Poet's Comment: This was after a year had passed since Marjory's wedding when she had become a mother.

Barbara in 1989

I said to the child who looked into my eyes,
Come let's play in the sun and the sand.
So we ran to the beach with laughing and shouts
So happy and free, without any doubts.

I said to the girl whom I'd taught what I knew
Why did you lie, what good could it do?
But she wouldn't reply and she wouldn't confess,
And all she could do was to weep and repress.

I said to the woman, before I give more
Please tell me the truth now, that's all I implore.
But the time was too late and she'd long shut the gate,
So she went on her way with her soul filled with hate.

And whether she's happy or hurting or sad,
I hope she remembers the words of her Dad.
And one day I pray, that God's Grace will break through,
And we'll walk on the sand and our love will renew.

First Memories *(2001)*

My first memories were optimistic,
Yet I was very ill.
Happy thoughts in the midst of trouble.
Twas my life in preview, in miniature.
I wonder is this the way it is?
We start out the way we are going to be.

The Red Pedal Car on the floor at the foot of my bed,
I felt the concern of my parents, their sense of relief.
That car was love at first sight for me,
I pedaled all over the garden, at the front, down the slope
To the garage and round to the stable,
Eventually down the steep path to the apple trees near the river.

It was the first time I felt loved by my father,
A tangible sign, a convincing evidence.
Mother's love I knew by instinct.
That's the way it was throughout my life with them,
I think that the way we are loved at first is the way it's going to be,
One by instinct, one by acts.

Hame-Gaun *(2001)*

As frae distant Bharat's shores he cam
Wi' hopes uplifted in his hert,
Lang miles o'er land and sea forgot,
A wee bit mission hoose he saucht.

Fu twa years bye hid passed awa
Ne'er wird nor scriff frae hame ava,
An nu the but and ben he'd funt
His guid-wife staundin oot the front.

She stood wi' bairnies three ahint her,
A weel-willan, fronty, frowdie, flichter.
Aince fur a wee he thocht twas true.
Neist morn he kent the pain anew.

Poet's Comment: A memory in the Doric (Doric was/is, another word for the Scots tongue)

Bill Robertson

Canis Lupus and Ursus Maritimus *(2002)*

The wolf and the bear
Lie each in his lair,
Using modern means
To unite the two scenes.

It's undoubtedly wise
And need not surprise,
That each has his way
To know just what to say.

Their special thoughts betimes they share
It's what they do, the wolf and the bear.

Poet's Comment: Just a thought between my son Greg and me.

Villanelle for Christine *(2009)*

A gentle maid, so warm and friendly
Always trusting and kind-hearted
She faced the world alone and bravely.

A tender flower that blossoms early
Demands of one a cautious tread
A gentle maid, so warm and friendly.

Intuitive, far-sightedly
Determined strong when all is said
She faced the world alone and bravely.

Approaching people helpfully
She soon learned how to make ones bread
A gentle maid, so warm and friendly.

A daughter's years are gone and quickly
And quietly comes a time to wed.
She faced the world alone and bravely.

Mature, a woman married lately
Is gone to golden years ahead.
A gentle maid, so warm and friendly
She faced the world alone and bravely.

Toast to the Bride *(2009)*

Dear daughter here with people all
How happy is this day
When from afar in early fall
We come to bless your way.

Born in far off Asia
You soon moved to the West
And later came to Canada
The land you love the best.

And now in this third continent
You've settled down to share
Both work and life and be content
It is a blessing rare.

Your roots are Scots and Irish kings
And Anglo-Saxon too
With Norse and French and Flemish wings
And ancient Scythian Jews.

So guided by your intuition
You chose to bind your honour
To one whose noble name is Shane
So now you're Chris O'Connor.

Please now do fill your glass and stand
For those we love the most
And now from all across the land
Let's drink a royal toast!

Poet's Comment: Written at the time my daughter Christine's wedding in Ottawa.

Pantoum for Greg *(2009)*

My son, my son, my only son
Your mother's son, to her most dear
Soon after when your life began
I knew and felt you would be near.

As child and boy you showed a flair
To work all day with tools and wood
It seemed it could be your career
To build upon this aptitude.

To work all day with tools and wood
And then to mathematics skill
To build upon this aptitude
You worked and studied with a will.

And then to mathematics skill
A computer science expert to be
You worked and studied with a will
an engineering Masters you.

A computer science expert to be
I knew and felt you would be near
an engineering Masters you
My son, my son, my only son.

Villanelle for Billy Stull *(2009)*

Early came and early went
Never happy, never sure
Oh was his life really meant?

Was he someone different
Or was there something not quite pure?
Early came and early went.

In early youth he was content
His mother's love did reassure
Oh that his life was really meant!

But other siblings then were sent
Which made him feel he was impure
Early came and early went.

And then to anger he gave vent
But violence never was a cure
Oh was his life really meant?

He never thought he could repent
Of what his victim did endure
Early came and early went
Oh was his life really meant?

Sonnet for Dad *(2009)*

My father's rule was duty to serve both king and country
In World War I he fought at Mons, survived and lived to tell the tale
But he wouldn't tell the details, too many dead said he,
"I was just lucky for all the true heroes died in the hail
Of bullets and shells with their bodies in pieces, their faces in slime."
After nine years of service as a regular soldier his career was all set
But his father destroyed it and said that his duty to him was prime.
When World War II broke out he made sure all his duties were met
For he knew that to meet Hitler's threat meant that all must respond to the call
After seven years of war and his duty well done he retired with a senior rank.

His children and wife, his parents and sisters he helped each one and all
But they gave little thanks for his dutiful life and preferred what he left in the bank.

Bill Robertson

Sonnet to Mother *(2009)*

My mother was a lady fair
With big blue eyes and jet-black hair.
Up until I hit teen-age
Hugging me was all the rage.
But then there came a different shift
That even then I found quite strange
She wouldn't touch me in a gift
So always I kept out of range.
There came a time in later life
I realized she had a hex
About her role as father's wife
In very truth she hated sex.

But Mummy dear you did your best
And now in heaven take your rest.

Poet's Comment: We are what we are. A thought still fresh thirty years after mother passed away.

Terranova Tete-A-Tete *(2009)*
A Pantoum

We gathered there to meet and chat
And some of us had never seen
So many that were sleek and fat
Though one or two were mean and lean.

And some of us had never seen
Each other for so many years
Though one or two were mean and lean
and saddened by remembered tears.

Each other for so many years
In distant places far apart
Though one or two were mean and lean
their memory a bitter dart.

In distant places far apart
Old disappointments, hurtful times
Their memory a bitter dart
And yet we hope for better climes.

Old disappointments, hurtful times
Of conversations we regret
And yet we hope for better climes
Where each one prays, forgive, forget.

Where each one prays, forgive, forget
With many that were sleek and fat
Of conversations we regret
We gathered there to meet and chat.

Poet's Comment: An after wedding house party, stirring old memories, yet hope for the future.

Villanelle for Toby *(2009)*

Most special friend we ever knew
Holds in our hearts a much loved place
Our Toby dog so loyal and true.

German shepherd, Collie too
A credit to her mountain race
Most special friend we ever knew.

So gentle, kind, yet on her cue
A guard so fearsome none could face
Our Toby dog so loyal and true.

As hunter there were very few
Who could in chasing her outpace
Most special friend we ever knew.

Of people she knew a thing or two
Her judgments wise, none could efface
Our Toby dog so loyal and true.

To meet again we hope to do
Somewhere maybe in outer space
Most special friend we ever knew
Our Toby dog so loyal and true.

Poet's Comment: Toby was a wonderful German Shepherd, Border Collie, Coyote dog. The best dog I ever knew. She passed away in 1980 and I still remember her twenty-four years later.

Villanelle for Janie *(2009)*

Janie Limond long does she reside
Where students came to learn to play
In stately home that e'er is called "Hillside".

And oft in evening times did she confide
At length with brother Tom and sister Fay
Where Janie Limond long did there reside.

And other friendly folk were much inclined
To chat for hours and sometimes come to stay
In stately home that e'er is called "Hillside".

An Ayrshire lady fills us all with pride
In all she's done o'er years and many a day
Yes Janie Limond long will she reside.

Through many years she sang in choirs refined
With practiced skill she led the Scottish play
In stately home that e'er is called "Hillside".

And now as fruitful decades still unwind
With cheerful voice and ready wit, we pray
That Janie Limond long years there reside
In stately home that e'er is called "Hillside".

Poet's Comment: Janie is our long-time friend in Scotland still going strong at a hundred years old.

Pantoum for Jack Stewart *(2009)*

He was a great and noble soul
Long past gone but still inspiring
As one to choose the higher role
And I to far-off doctoring.

Long past gone but still inspiring
A man with vision for his day
And I to far-off doctoring
For struggling youth he knew the way.

A man with vision for his day
His word his look inspired each man
For struggling youth he knew the way
And led them all to say I can.

His word his look inspired each man
As one to choose the higher role
And led them all to say I can
He was a great and noble man.

Poet's Comment: The prime mentor of my youth, Jack was a giant among men, the finest one I ever knew. Queen Elizabeth II awarded Jack an Order of the British Empire (OBE), but I think it should have been a Knighthood.

Villanelle for Margie and Ken *(2009)*

Margie and Ken in Sturgeon Bay
Happy we came to their welcoming door
So kind and so helpful in every way.

How can we ever their kindness repay
Our talks and our travels were good to the core
Margie and Ken in Sturgeon Bay.

Remembering the sights on lovely Green Bay
And times of good friendship, our spirits will soar
So kind and so helpful in every way.

In Clinics and Rotary they work every day
Of dedication and service none could do more
Margie and Ken in Sturgeon Bay.

Two souls for whose happiness we always will pray
That good things and good times will continually pour
So kind and so helpful in every way.

Poet's Comment: On a visit to Sturgeon Bay, Wisconsin, to Sally's long-time friend, Margie.

My Old Dad *(2010)*

Long dead but not forgotten he
Who lies at peace in Shettles way.
Not battlefields that he did see
Where comrades fought and died each day.

The shattered trees of Belgian Mons
to him a baptism of fire.
For many other Scottish sons
it proved to be a funeral pyre.

He thus survived the Kaiser's threat
To fight in freezing mud was sent
Then later to the Sinai's dust
With deadly weapons then he must.

And once again escaped alive
While fighting in the desert sand
But sadly few did there survive
His brother's death it did demand.

His father ruled him as before
A wife and business he must take
The family's comfort to ensure
While his career he must forsake.

In years between the wars he toiled
His back was up against the wall
Then Hitler's evil anger boiled
Once more he answered duty's call.

To fight and die he ere was willing
Though oft at risk, t'was not his fate
To die in war's gigantic killing
The hand of death would have to wait.

His role this time was all defense
Of Air Force stations from attack
Including Gas if it commenced
He organized a powerful flack.

His midnight drills on Anti-Gas
Were famous, feared by one and all
They were the best within their class
And my old Dad stood straight and tall.

In six long years the war was won
He'd worked right through without a break
They thanked him for a job well done
all for king and country's sake.

Back to the business after the war
The trade was changing mighty fast
He sold the shops for less than par
happy to see it all going past.

Air Training in the West he led
And traveling towards the setting sun
With courage bore the cancer's spread
And ne'er a word, save to his son.

As life was moving to its close
He eyed the future still with hope
Ignoring clouds of gathering woes
Made no complaint, nor cry, nor mope.

Still looking to the following day
And having nothing left to say
He smiling shook the hand of death
And silent breathed his final breath.

Poet's Comment: Forty-five years after his passing. A final thought of Dad.

Greg's in Gear *(2012)*
A Villanelle

A man with a vision is a man on a mission,
He sees what is needed and comes up with a plan.
He makes up his mind and comes to decision.

At first he reviews all the facts with precision,
And finds out where all the problems began.
A man with a vision is a man on a mission.

Some of the issues he found caused some friction,
With tact and diplomacy were solved to a man.
He makes up his mind and comes to decision.

Academics are prone to resist change on occasion,
It takes skill and energy to create what you can.
A man with a vision is a man on a mission.

Success is achieved when plans come to fruition,
Rewards are received with a smiling deadpan.
He makes up his mind and comes to decision.

Yes, Greg is the guy they need for completion,
Who collects all the projects and leads from the van.
A man with a vision is a man on a mission,
He makes up his mind and comes to decision.

The Benevolent Bear *(2013)*

On Conestoga's Board of Governors he is voted a member,
His term commences the first of September.
With a new role to fill there'll be much on his plate,
A province-wide network which he'll integrate.

The Benevolent Bear has emerged from his lair,
As always he moves with infinite care.
His ideas resound with the sound of success,
His suggestions abound and always impress.

Wisdom and reason will clear their illusions,
Leading to great and successful conclusions.
So look out you problems you'd better not fail,
Or you'll end up in trouble with a bear on your tail!

A Hundred Glorious Years *(2013)*

Janie Limond has reached her hundred,
Ever true and ere well-bred.
A lady of prodigious power,
Her time has come, her Royal Hour.

The Queen has sent congratulations,
Giving Janie great sensations.
The value of her lengthy days,
Cannot be measured, just amaze.

A Limond lady strong and tall,
Janie will outdo them all.
Wherever one goes, far or near,
Will not be found, her like or peer.

Connie *(2013)*

I can't believe you're ninety-three
It isn't true, it cannot be!
If you'd said almost forty-two
Then I'd agree that could be true.

The Governor's Grant *(2014)*

Governor Greg never says can't
When he sets out to get a government grant.
He toiled all day and many a night
Until the approach he devised was quite right.

The objective was clear; manufacturing studies
Not vague thought up schemes by some dull fuddie-duddies.
He knows what is needed and what to reject
And how to promote a worthwhile project.

When next at the Board he announces success
The room will resound with the sounds of a "Yes!"
As they realize with joy they'd appointed a "Bear"
And agreed one-and-all twas an answer to prayer.

Sally

To Sally on Her Birthday *(1975)*

Strong, warm and beautiful a flower
Blooming in the desert she came
into the aridness of his life.

As the smiling sun reflects its splendor
On the red rock hills,
So will her true love bring warmth and light
to the shadows of his inner self.

As a miner sifts the precious ores of the mountains
So will she discover hidden wealth within his depths
And enrich all their life.

But why he wonders is this happening to him
And finding no answer murmurs a prayer of gratitude.

Poet's Comment: This poem's first lines defines a key turning point in my life.

Sally O'Stool *(1975)*

There once was a lady called Sally O'Stool
She came from "The Island" in legend tis told.
While thinking of marriage and the pride of her kin
She planned to be neither too fat nor too thin.

She followed a regime whose effect put the brunt
On the problem she saw of excess at the front,
Five pounds she was sure she had lost for a fact,
But in truth it had just gone around to the back!

Poet's Comment: Sally's maiden name was 'Stull'. This humorous poem was written as she prepared for our marriage.

The Appointed Hour *(1975)*

Oh joy that comes from Him above,
Between two souls in tune with love.
That love not as the wanton's toy
Is born of God, a heavenly joy.

Oh peace that stills the troubled soul
And spans the Earth from pole to pole
To each there comes an appointed hour
For us to know its ageless power.

The Autumn of a Year *(1975)*

In the autumn of a year I remember,
On a morning bright, clear, like the blue of your eyes,
We looked into our hearts and knew it was true.
The day passed light as a butterfly on gossamer wings
finds her way home,
In the evening we knew that life is hope and love is the way.

In the autumn of a year I remember,
A windswept night and rain beating in my face,
Twas then we discovered the barb of love's pain,
Yet knowing all along we could not complain.
A cold fearful anguish crept into our hearts.
In the autumn of a year I remember.

In the autumn of a year I remember,
I found you again in the sun.
Like a flower whose bloom awaits th' appointed hour,
Your petals, tender, exquisite,
Delicately opening to a loving touch
And I knew our lives had just begun.
In the autumn of a year I remember.

Autumn Leaves *(1975)*

Autumn leaves growing red on the trees in my garden,
And winter still to come before the spring.
How will we wait so long to be together
To feel love's sweet song within us sing?

Winter's herald winds strip off soft leaves as they blow
Leaving only the bark naked to the sky.
But our love will stand firm in the winter's snow
And our hope will endure like a sigh.

Suddenly Spring will arrive in our lives
Buds will grow green and leaves start to quiver
The sap rising strong reassures life survives.
Foretaste of joy we'll know then forever.

Summer will come and its blossoms appear
And I'll stand at your side 'neath their glow
We'll pledge each our troth for all there to hear
And the whole wide world round then will know.

Reaching Out *(1975)*

As a flower seeks the warmth of the sun
So does my soul reach out for your love.
As the surge of the incoming tide
So your love engulfs my being.

Longing *(1975)*

If I but once could feel the gentle clasp
Of those dear fingers round me, firm
Or sigh and cry with you in tender ecstasy of union sweet divine.
If treasure once again the fleeting moments bemusing bliss
When time is lost in soul uplifting love enraptured kiss,
Or passions drained, again to turn and love with unabated fire and mutual joy,
Till love and life and you and I are ever one in our sweet world of dreams.

Seeing Your Photograph *(1975)*

My darling it is my delight
To see that friendly eye so bright
Neath gently arching eye-brows fair
Those neatest bows of smoothest hair.
Warm lines that frame those gentle eyes
That e'er my heart do hypnotise.

Thy smiling multi-dimpled cheek
I long to kiss, my lips do seek
So soft and full and warmly tender
My passions all to them surrender.

Soft, soft that cheek and tender ear
To kiss beneath gold crowning hair,
And hold again thy head so dear
Caress so gently, hold thee near.

Sally's blue eyes and radiant smile
Renew my faith, my heart beguile.
Her love that doth my being enfold
In perfect peace my soul doth hold.

Since first we met you've captured all my being
A happy slave I am and will remain;
Whose only wish to serve each noble feeling
Which from your heart proceeds like gentle rain.

Winter *(1976)*

It is winter, the silent snow clings to the trees,
And looking out I think only of you, the spring and summer leaves.

The sun shines bright, sparkling the icy tracery of the branches,
But I long to see the warmth of the love in your eyes, renewing my soul.

The wind trembles in the dark trees like the rustle of your walk,
And closing my eyes I feel the sweetness of your presence.

Waiting *(1976)*

When green buds are opening,
With joyful faces upturned to the hope-filled rain,
I'll open a door and find you waiting there.

When winter winds are blowing
And there is no comfort but the cold, distant snow,
There is no life to see, only waiting for the Spring.

Poet's Comment: These poems were composed not in any particular order during 1975 and 1976
were part of my offered thoughts to Sally leading up to our marriage in September 1976.

Sally is Coming *(1980)*

Lightning flashes, thunder roars
Blood and sweat exudes my pores.
Hither, thither see me dashing
In among the puddles splashing.
Suddenly the storm is past,
Sally is coming, peace at last!

Poet's Comment: A brief statement of awareness and reassurance that Sally was completing her time in Ottawa when we had moved to Bedford. That says it all.

SALLY *(2000)*

Into the world she came, too late for her mother.
It wasn't meant to be, not like her "early" brother!
Not black or red, but tow-white her hair,
And blue eyes beautiful beyond compare.

But angels standing round her little bed,
Bestowed on her a Gran instead,
Who guessed about her dogged fight,
To overcome dyslexia's blight.

The hell of words she could not spell,
And no one she could risk to tell,
With iron will she sought the prize,
Each word and page was memorized!

Her favorite place was in the trees,
Or with her doggie on her knees.
Words not needed to share these moments,
Just peaceful looks and silent comments.

Her elder brother, brat and bully,
Abusive, selfish, all unruly,
Filled her life with hurt and fear,
Except when Grandmama was near.

At ten with life still just as hard,
Her brother's child she had to guard.
With mother love the orphan tended,
So soon her childhood thus was ended.

Family problems came and went,
But Sally forged ahead, hell-bent.
Her school exams she did surmount
And so moved up to reach The Mount.

A nurse she set her sights to be,
And laboured long and mightily.
In language others never knew,
She and the Newfies formed their crew.

Twas soon she led the class in style,
Ne'er victim of some Sister's wile.
Her many ploys she planned with wit
Fulfilling all with nervy grit.

Good friends she had from East and West,
All knew that they by her were blest.
But others hearts were filled with gall,
They played their "tricks" in Montreal.

A Mount grad. Of the Sister's School,
A truly intellectual jewel.
Throughout her life she always rose,
To every challenge which arose.

Her Mount St. Vincent days now past,
She stuck her colours to the mast.
Nursing at the Infirmary,
Honouring Sister Assisi.

Thus just before her sixteenth year,
She boldly entered her career.
In those days nurses studied hard,
While also working in the ward.

Of many trials and tribulations,
In wards and after operations,
In skill no other could surpass her,
Not even Sister Catherine Peter.

She worked so hard with much endeavour,
That soon she passed her R.N. Degree.
Then on she went as she was clever,
And took an Honor's B.Sc.

But all this work revealed the signs,
Which sapped her strength too many times,
Of Lupus' kinds of aches and pain,
And off and on they still remain.

Then in nineteen sixty-five,
Her health, a little did revive,
And studying for a Diplomate,
In Nursing Teaching, she did rate.

At twenty-one she'd gained her crown,
Twas now a time to settle down.
A bold young man her hand did seek,
And soon she married at her peak.

So Sally Stull became a Linkert,
A Roman Catholic kind of convert.
From Popish clan to the Lutheran.
She never was sectarian!

For three short years at the N.S. she taught,
And once again her health was fraught.
But she remained both meek and mild,
And Lo! She quietly bore a child!

A bouncing boy, he came on time;
Big and strong, but quite refined.
He was baptized as Gregory,
But known as Greg to you and me.

Alas so soon a tragedy!
His Daddy disappeared, you see.
They never really found out why,
And so remains a timeless sigh.

But Sally knew she could not fret,
Although she was in crushing debt.
A lady, Queen in quality,
She still walked tall, for all to see.

Thus all alone in life she stood,
'Gainst cruel Fate and Fortune rude.
A better job became her mission,
Consultant to the great Commission!

In this task too she was a winner,
And did more work before her dinner,
Than all the others put together.
Oh my! But she was bright and clever.

While all this time though deep in debt,
She uttered no complaint or fret.
Keeping her budget ever tight,
And sometimes going without a bite.

Her manager was full of praise,
And recommended then a "raise".
Which he knew well was only fair,
But reckoned not on Mr. Hare.

Discouraged, tired and needing rest,
She got the chance to go out West.
The Yankees soon realized her worth,
And offered her a brand new berth.

The job was fine, the money good,
And so she did just what she should.
She said "Farewell" to Nova Scotia,
And then "Hullo" to Arizona!

So now she joined the Wilpitz crew,
At Marcus Lawrence Centre new.
Bob Sykes and Smitty were true friends,
And kept her up on all the trends.

Happy to be in South-West, she
Basked in the warmth of the sun.
Far from the cold of the Eastern Sea,
Safe in her home with her son.

The nights at home were quiet but dark,
A friend was needed with a bark.
Toby a German Shepherd Collie,
But also a rumped and tailed coyote!

Thus well-established she began,
To spread her wings to fullest span.
Within the wards, across the State,
What she did was all first rate.

All the good she did back then,
Would take a book to tell,
Of plans and projects done so well,
I hope one day she'll pen.

The days went by both fast and furious,
Greg was happy, Toby was curious.
Visitors came to bask in the sun,
And loved to see the Grand Canyon.

An admiring doctor came one day,
A diamond ring was in his hand.
He hoped that she would come away,
And wear for him a Wedding Band.

It took a year and more to achieve,
Then Arizona she did leave.
Greg and Toby and Sally "Ma",
All flew away to Ottawa.

In September nineteen-seventy-six,
The Twenty-fifth the date was fixed.
In St. Andrew's Kirk the happy pair,
Bill and Sally married there!

Bells Corner where they settled down,
It didn't take long to reach Downtown.
And Greg could go to school quite near.
The streets were quiet, there was no fear.

Twas Sally's turn to study too,
She traveled daily to Ottawa U.,
And passed her Master's in Health Administration,
A Johnson & Johnson Award sensation!

Next she studied at the C.N.A.,
Found foul corruption within it lay,
Which really upset old Mussalam,
Leaving her numb as well as "dumb".

Such brains they had to keep quite close,
A directorship they then proposed.
So Sally led the N.U.A.,
And made it run a "better" way.

Now Canada had Trudeau crowned,
And French he sent to Ottawa bound.
The leaders were a Quebec gang,
And ordered all to be "bilingue".

She must speak French or be maligned,
And leave all honest work behind.
She said she'd tell her French Grandma,
But twas too late, she said, "Ta Ta!"

And they moved to join B.E.C.,
There they worked and stewed like heck.
A thousand-bedded Centre planned,
But in the end the plan was canned!

So next they heaved a grateful sigh,
And headed off to P.E.I.,
To Sally's home, so green and clean,
As fine a place as ever's seen.

She reorganized the Mental Hosp.,
And had to fight a Fraser Wasp.
As ever she did just what she ought,
Clearing the chaos, with mighty swat!

Then next she made a Company,
Consisting just of her and me.
Contracts came in ones and twos,
Some to do and some refuse.

She read a ton of books back then,
From Enki on to Akhenaten.
And painted oils in healing tones,
Regrowing flesh on saddened bones.

United Way and Gus MacFarlane,
Contracts large and small she parleyed.
And ten years good and happy passed,
Long time enjoyed, but over fast.

But then old Willie did retire,
From years of Federal flame and fire.
To Lotus Land, four thousand miles,
They found a haven full of smiles.

Such happiness always comes with a price,
A mortgage large, that's not so nice.
Their home was big enough for three,
So Greg enrolled at U. of V.

They both were working paid and free,
On varied jobs from A to Z.
Then Sally found a sleazy job,
Aworkin' for the socialist mob.

To work for those you don't respect,
Is never easy to select.
Needs must when the Devil drives, tis' true,
She had to serve that Left-Wing zoo!

In nineteen Ninety-Nine she quit,
The Ministry it made one spit.
Retired with "five", a pension made,
And happy she that it was paid.

But just as all seemed at a peak,
Their condominium sprang a leak!
Repairs to cost three million two,
And now they didn't know what to do.

But Ian Lawson gave advice,
Which solved their problem in a trice.
At least that's what it seemed in part,
And certainly it was a start.

They then must rent their leaky condo
Buy a house, become a landlord.
To cover wholesale leak repairs,
And hopefully avoid night-mares.

Those evil bureaucratic lords,
Denied all blame for building flaws.
And paid the wily Barrett well,
Their truth evading lies to tell.

Yet they had hopes to stay alive,
And at the "Ridge" to strong survive.
So when the condo is repaired,
They hope to sell it, if they're spared.

Meantime Sally painted up a storm,
Three a week is just her norm.
This month the Art Show's coming up,
One day quite soon she'll win the Cup!

Now even Bill is drawing with pen,
And typing Bio now and then.
As Reiki Masters they commune,
Helping Sister to attune.

There's more to come they hope for sure,
And they'll be happy rich or poor.
Two souls who've found their true release,
And live in harmony and peace.

But Sally's life is still not old,
And all her story's not been told,
A Queen she'll reign for many a year.
In all the world there's not her peer!

Poet's Comment: Sally's life in rhyme.

Darling Sally *(2009)*
A Villanelle

Darling Sally Queen of Wisdom
Island girl with the strawberry curl
Goddess true of Intuition.

Consultant to the Health Commission
There she did her flag unfurl
Darling Sally Queen of Wisdom.

To Arizona she did roam
Gave Marcus Lawrence quite a whirl
Goddess true of Intuition.

In Ottawa she made a union
Wedded and a much loved girl
Darling Sally Queen of Wisdom.

Next she proved her constitution
PhD from way Down Under
Goddess true of Intuition.

An author now she ruled a kingdom
Her Pebble book a shining pearl
Darling Sally Queen of Wisdom
Goddess true of Intuition.

Sonnet to a Friend *(2009)*

A late unwanted mother's child
Who early found her challenge, Words!
In streams of jumping, jumbled cords
Meaningless and fearsome, wild!
And none could help her cruel plight
Alone she had to find a way
By steel-like effort every day
To nobly face this life-long fight.

One day she met a man who cared
But did not know her secret sorrow
That had to wait a new tomorrow
When each to each their soul's they bared.
In life its true one needs a friend
To share life's burdens to the end.

My Best Friend *(2012)*

My friend and dearest friend of all, my wife,
No wiser person have I known in life.
I see her sitting, resolute in toil,
To daily duty ever true and loyal.

With words her life-long battle never ceases
As captive ones from bondage she releases.
By reading, writing, speaking unabating,
Holding an enemy at bay who's ever waiting.

What trials in her life she e'er was bearing,
From teachers void of knowledge, love or caring.
Her clever Grandma knew that something ailed her,
And tried each day to solve her odd behaviour.

Her mother, who God knows had caused the discord,
And from its birth her child she never favoured.
What guilt she should have felt throughout her years,
From smoke and drink, to cause such stress and tears.

To hate the child that she herself created,
What hellish fate for her is now awaited.
How many long and cruel incarnations,
Her soul will weep in endless lamentations.

It's nice to think someone will take the blame,
In fact they'll say it's really 'Such a shame'.
Dyslectics must accept and soldier on,
For few there are who care or think upon.

Best Friends *(2013)*

I love you she said, on Valentine's Day,
For when I talk you always hear
You know the things I can't just say,
Or whether it came out quite clear.

When I reach out you're always there,
To anticipate my every need,
Or what at times I would prefer,
You ably then my thoughts can read.

When I laugh you laugh with me,
It doesn't matter what or whether,
We know where we both will be,
It's any place we're both together.

She's my partner, my best friend,
That's the way it's going to end.

The Serpent Queen *(2013)*

Its April 9th two thousand thirteen
News has just come to the great Serpent Queen
That sales of her book are already two score
And when current accounting comes in there'll be more.

The Serpent Queen has done it, I knew that she would,
Be a first class author who was bound to be good.
She has proved she could do it and is now on her way,
To a wonderful future, a new dawning day.

Queen Sally *(2013)*

When reaching three-score years and ten
You'd best forget why, where or when.
For now you sit upon a throne,
Supreme you reign, but not alone.

Exalted now, you are elite,
A Doctor, author, quite complete.
Before you now all worlds await,
The Serpent's longed-for publishing date.

But long before you see that date
Your mind will search through Tara's Gate.
Hoping that by next Samhain
Wondrous knowledge you will gain.

With Angi you had made a plan
That she'd intuit all she can.
Sirona too will give you aid,
On how this world of Magic's made.

And soon new mysteries will unfold,
Ne'er in this world have yet been told.
You are the Queen by whom 'tis said
The Celtic's Serpent's tales were made.

There's no one who by quiet reflection,
Can make the Magic world's connection.
A story-teller of repute,
You are a wondrous golden fruit.

The Serpent Druid Queen *(2014)*

The Serpent Queen from far away
Somewhere in the Milky Way.
Multi-million years ago,
Her special genes began to flow.

And from that planet's primal place
Began the first Druidical race.
Across the ages, times long past
Wisdom won from first to last.

Take me now through Tara's Gate
Where pilgrims meet their happy fate.
I'll enter then the life serene
And meet the Serpent Druid Queen.

Philosophy

Winter Hope *(1969)*

Naked black the maple stands, its bony
Limbs uplifted to an azure sky.
Through its thicket, dimpled glistening far below
The sea too awaits the winter's ice.

These silent symbols faithful stand
Sure in their Creator's hand
Their patient vigil gives us hope.

Poet's Comment: Composed in March 1969 still hoping that the family would follow me to Canada.

Not Sentiment *(1970s)*

Blinks cold between the fleeting clouds
The staring moon aloof glides on,
Nor heeds, tight-packed, the crouching trees
Black, jungle-veiled with silvered leaves.

And deep within the glistening shroud
Like monstrous vile imagined things
The living dead forgotten lie
Nor hear their tortured stifled cry.

In fetid mud they sprawl and squirm
Poor damned souls long done with hoping
Not theirs to ask the reason why
Yet somewhere still remains a sigh.

While life remains hope stirs within
God may reprieve their loathsome sin
Faith lingers long where once it bloomed
And love goes on sweet bitter fruit.

A bearded sage despairing cries
They're gone, consumed, no soul survives
Yet how can he who's known true peace
Have faith in hell-begotten souls?

Can one whose years knew peaceful joys
Yet understand the spawn of hell?
How can they see who never saw
Or hope for those their minds abhor?

No! Youth's doubting twisted, troubled soul
Must seek an answer of its own.
Not sentiment, Edwardian tears
But hopeful faith in that Unseen.

Poet's Comment: This was composed soon after I arrived in Halifax, Canada in the dead of a Canadian winter, one evening looking out of a window in the basement of the home in which I had found temporary accommodation until the family arrived from Scotland. There had been no letters from my wife and no indication as to when or even if they would be coming. But the main theme of the poem was my concern of the way modern youth was too often choosing the less worthy path in life.

Self Confidence *(1974)*

Waiting for action before a big game,
It was there in our youth and its still just the same.
Savouring play and what needs to be done,
Tense in the gut at the thought of a run.

The game's just the same though it's different in ways,
The stakes are much higher and we're shorter on days.
We'll try to succeed in the dash for the line,
And taste the sweet richness of victory's wine.

But we're in there to fight and we know what to do,
If we just get the ball we know we'll come through.
We've just got to be sure right deep down inside,
And then we'll come through on the crest of the tide.

Poet's Comment: A thought based on my days playing rugby in the senior League of the Scottish Rugby Union, as I handled the Challenges of being a senior medical civil servant in the federal government.

Courtesy *(1974)*

Of courtesy it is much less
Than courage of heart or holiness.
Yet in my walk it seems to me
That the Grace of God is in courtesy.

Truth *(1980)*

Out in the void in a place all unknown,
I search for the truth where it stands all alone.
To be humble, obedient, to answer the call,
Is that what we're here for, till death reaches us all?

Yes it's really enough just to know we belong,
That we're part of the whole and singing in tune with the endless God song.

There's nothing so simple as knowing your part
If you follow your reason with faith in your heart.
Give pride not a place, nor ambition its will,
And peace and contentment you'll have to your fill.

Poet's Comment: A thought reinforcing my beliefs in how to live in a world seeming to lose its values.

We All Die *(1999)*

Why so interested in tragedy,
So little enthused by happiness?
Finding a Muse in melancholy
And inspiration in distress.

Then life is sad and filled with woes
Yes, in the end they take their toll
Trees do withstand the blasting storm
Yet each has scars to call its own.

All living things do end in death
Sooner or later they all must die
To leave no mark, or word, or sigh.

Such cruel fate and bitter end
It fascinates the mortal mind
Tis hall-mark of our human-kind.

Boomer's Corporate Morality *(2002)*

What price is corporate morality?
I think I'd just prefer a cup of tea.
Ah tell me not of WorldCom's doom,
Or why is Enron in its tomb.

I suppose its time to clean things up.
D'you think we've time for another cup?
Yea sure, let's really let it all hang out,
And anyway who's keeping count?

No, I feel there's been enough disruptions
Heh, look at all our great stock options!
They're running into umpteen billions,
I guess we're both worth ten gezillions!

What's that they say it's not that way?
They're going to take us both away!!
Though we both tried to help investors,
The judge says we're just foul infestors!

Take 'em away, expand the gaols!

Poet's Comment: A thought about two wealthy fat cats discussing the Enron crisis.

Meditative Soliloquy *(2005)*

Anon the odd paranoiac thought,
To make believe what one ought not.

Three score and ten, plus four am I,
Too early yet for me to die.
And yet the odd delusional thought,
Can make believe what one ought not.

I don't intend to toddle off,
As victim to a smoker's cough,
Or pigging on cholesterol,
Get heart attack, no not at all!

Human Love *(2009)*

Love's passion youth's consuming fire
The ageless search to find a mate
Whose beauty fills the heart's desire
And leads man on to fickle fate.
Sometimes when the bloom is off her
Once rampant stallion's blood is cooled
The waning charm him does deter
And love's sweet mystery seems fooled.

But if with wisdom he reflects
Love's deeper values comprehends
And passion's fleeting joys rejects
Then heavenly understanding lends
Enduring powers of true devotion
Acceptance, friendship's heavenly potion.

Sonnet on Truth and Justice *(2009)*

Politics they say is the art of the possible
Based on whoever has power and control.
Whether that's fair is not open to quibble
It's all just a question of reaching ones goal.
The Romans in Europe, the Normans in England
With savage intent and ruthless suppression
Defined truth and justice by regal command
Establishing power with crushing repression.
One hopes there'll be times when democracy wins
And dictators' ambitions are brought to the ground
But mostly the bad guys get off with their sins
The halls of the powerful with laughter abound.

While wars and vain strife may not ever quite cease
A quiet resignation will always give peace.

Cosmic Delusion *(2013)*

Death is but a new beginning
On the way to heaven winging
Leading to an astral life
Far from misery and strife.

We hope in time for endless bliss
That goal we know we must not miss.
Though incarnations come and go
We ere will seek the heavenly glow.

Its true there is some real confusion
On what we know of cosmic delusion
Or where we go when life is o'er
We realize there's much, much more.

God the only non-vibration
He it is who planned creation.
From universe to smallest cell
Vibration is their common shell.

Each item has its own vibration
Unique within its own equation.
Stone and wood, water and gas
Each vibrate within their class.

All of life is an illusion
What we seek is a solution.
The answer is the heavenly kiss
Of meditating Eternal Bliss.

Modern Middle Class Morality *(2013)*

When I was young and still quite small,
I didn't foresee how far standards would fall.
Before I was forty and still quite young,
It came as a shock and it really stung.

After I came back from years in the East,
I heard about Woodstock's bacchanalian feast.
Middle-class morality had slid down the drain.
The world that I knew had gone quite insane.

My Presbyterian world of quiet moderations,
Couldn't handle a world of free sexual relations.
Cheating at school and stealing from malls,
Slacking at work and scratching on walls.

The position of society's classes in history,
Has always been clear and never a mystery.
The toffs above and the workers below,
With the middle class the in-between row.

When a nation aspires to become a democracy,
It needs to get rid of existing autocracy,
Which might be a ruthless family-led monarchy,
Or a workers police-state Communist oligarchy.

The moral values of a nation,
Need people with an education,
Who'll work and strive from morn til night,
Until they've got the standards right.

The upper class with power and wealth,
Are not concerned with people's health.
As long as their workers toil all day,
They're happy having fun and play.

The lower class must work to eat,
And now and then they have to cheat.
Some Labour Unionists breed hate,
And seek to create a Fascist state.

Only the middle class answers the call,
It is the class that does it all.
Leading their nation to a higher morality,
Creating a socio-political totality.

Old Middle Class Morality *(2013)*

I remember as a child
We followed Jesus meek and mild.
At home or school on Sunday morn
We sang how He a child was born.

We knelt to say our prayers at night
And asked for strength to do the right.
At school we had to toe the line
And be there prompt at ten to nine.

We learned that life was not just play
Not getting always our own way.
We knew we had to share the work
And no one was allowed to shirk.

After school on each week day
Girls and boys went out to play.
After supper before bed
There was homework to be read.

Our family shared the breakfast table
All together strong and stable.
Young and old we formed a team
Some gave sugar, others cream.

At sports we played both hard and fair
Though doing our best, applause was rare.
To be a star was not our dream
We strove to win by being a team.

We knew we had to earn a living
In life twas not just getting but giving.
We always said our Please and Thank You s
Carefully minding our Ps and Qs.

God's Ten Commandments we avowed
No stealing, covetousness, lies, allowed.
Respecting parents, loving others
Loving God above our mothers.

Quantum Jump *(2013)*

Omnipresent light of Spirit
Evolves, sustains all existing life.
Creative vibration is that life,
It is the word the sound of life.

Every entity in the world
By ego's conscious mind is made.
Matter remains as pure possibility,
Until that mind thinks actuality.

The shimmering waves of pure possibility
Can only be changed by a mind's creativity.
But when the observer withdraws his attention,
The wave function collapses as a quantum jump.

Religion

A Morning Prayer *(1954)*

I thank Thee Father for peace and rest
Another night with sleep was blest
For opportunities to serve
I pray for energy and nerve.

Fill me Lord with faith supreme
With love and hope a balanced team.
Peace and joy, truth and courage
In all of these my soul engage.

To give rather than be given,
Forgive rather than being forgiven
Console rather than being consoled
Understand rather than being understood.

To love rather than to be loved
And with attentiveness and patience
To gentleness and kindliness
Reach wisdom on to perfect peace.

Efface those vain imaginings
Suppressing impulse, checking desires
And by a powerful self-control
Maintain self-mastery of my soul.

Always do that which is just
Meeting foes with mercy first.
And when life gives me power control
Bless me with a humble soul.

Teach me the path of delayed gratification
For that which is real complete dedication
Ever responsible for my own life
Balancing behaviour, omitting all strife.

Show forth a genuine love for others
Seeking the best for your sisters and brothers
Filled with God's love and reaching omniscience
Of the highest spiritual good in essence.

Transported beyond this earthly world
Where flags and banners fly unfurled
I take an evolutionary leap
Far into infinity's boundless deep.

In the multitude of words there wanteth not sin
The wise who refraineth his lips will win.
Before my mouth set a watch O Lord
That my lips express the truth of Thy Word.

Poet's Comment: I have said this prayer every morning for the past fifty-nine years.

The Future for Anglicans *(2003)*

As the Anglicans said to the Pope
We think you are now our last hope.
If you'll keep our gay priests, and most of our feasts
We'll soon remarry or maybe elope.

Anglican Conformity *(2009)*

If you wish to be reborn
Anglican you'll want to be
You must learn how to conform.

When you rise up every morn
Always genuflect your knee
If you wish to be reborn.

From the day that you were born
It is best that you foresee
You must learn how to conform.

When you hear the morning horn
Sip a cup of Earl Grey tea
If you wish to be reborn.

You may feel a bit forlorn
But you soon will come to see
You must learn how to conform.

When your spirit seems to yearn
Then you know you've found the key
If you wish to be reborn
You must learn how to conform.

Poet's Comment: My brief sojourn among the Anglicans has finally convinced me that constant ritualistic conformity and a diet of nothing but endless Prayer Book repetition, cannot sustain my Presbyterian soul.

Call To Mission *(2009)*
A Villanelle

A call to go and join the flow
To rid the world of grief and pain
And seeming sure of where to go

To take up arms against the foe
And never did I go for gain
A call to go and join the flow

You'd think I really had to know
That what I'd done might be insane
And seeming sure of where to go

To reap one always first must sow
For otherwise it's all in vain
A call to go and join the flow

One should not have a wife in toe
Especially in the Tropic rain
Yet seeming sure of where to go

Your answer whether con or pro
Is key before you board the plane
A call to go and join the flow
And seeming sure of where to go.

Poet's Comment: A look back at my missionary decision fifty-five years ago.

Health

Reiki Till Ah Drop *(2000)*

Ah'm a Reiki wreck, yes Ah am by heck,
Abeamin' an ascannin' from your toes to your neck,
With a Choku rei and a Sei he ki,
Oh God please have mercy on me!

Ah'm a Therapeute, yes A'hm kinda cute,
With ma healin' hands ah sure am a beaut!
With a hon sha ze sho nen,
A transmit the power of ten!

As a Distance Healer A'hm a wheeler-dealer,
First the symbols then to beamin', an Ah think that Ahm adreamin,
But Ah keep on concentratin' an it keeps me all elatin',
For Ah know that dude's ahealin' an he's got that certain feelin!

Blockage Blues *(2009)*

One day my bladder and my bowel
Gave out a loud and piteous howl
What monstrous, vile a thing is this
I cannot even S--- or P---?

But Cowichan to my aid appeared
Sir Bladder Bill my block he speared
And good Sir Peter's measured plan
My rescue from foul pain began.

Then days of Sitz and Metamucil
I followed long without refusal
Until one day I took a hop
With hope to check in for an Op.

My namesake froze me from the waist
And kept me safe from pain's dark taste
Then skilled Sir Peter did me upend
And swiftly solved my shattered end.

Next day twas home to convalesce
Enjoying my wife's sweet tenderness
While sitting on a rubber ring
Twas Dr. Paul's advised thing.

Later when some time had passed
Sir Bladder Bill was unsurpassed
Removing then that wicked gland
Which seeks one's vital path's command.

For all my doctors' skillful care
There's nothing else which can compare
And words seem lacking gratitude
For constant care that was so good.

The nurses' care I'll ne'er forget
Their names will be remembered yet
Like Julie, Sarah, Liz and Gail
To them and more I say, "All Hail."

Bill Robertson

To all of Cowichan's staff give praise
For all their work in all their ways
I've seen a lot in eighty years
And Cowichan deserves, "Three Cheers."

Villanelle to Ezetrol *(2009)*

The side effects of Ezetrol
Were growing worse both night and day
It helped poor Sally not at all.

First it caused a need to crawl
Her tingling feet caused much dismay
The side effects of Ezetrol.

The next effect which did befall
Was muscle pain which I must say
It helped poor Sally not at all.

Headache too it came to call
Its presence clearly to convey
The side effects of Ezetrol.

Some tummy pain she did recall
Which came but once then went away
It helped poor Sally not at all.

To lower her cholesterol
She seeks another way to stay
The side effects of Ezetrol
It helped poor Sally not at all.

A Northern Hospital *(2011)*

A health board is trying to play games in the North,
Hired a consultant who didn't know what she should do,
But produced a report which was useless, of virtually no worth,
Which the hospital staff studied and gave their review.

Now three months later there's still no replies,
Just another report by the person who only knows squat.
This is clearly an insult to all of the hard-working guys
And it seems that Board staff are engaged in a plot.

Some accountant on high is concocting what he thinks is a plan,
Which will force the hospital people to give up the game,
But he knows if not careful it could all hit the fan,
And end up destroying his fame and illustrious name.

The things that are lacking from Boomers today are the facts,
Which can clarify problems and lead to solutions, The Truth!

A Grumpy Day in November *(2011)*

On this miserable day best keep away!
What it looks like outside, I'd better not say.
We don't feel like a chat, it might be a pain,
As our thoughts are quite mixed by the wind and the rain.

I'm feeling the pinch, old age's not a cinch.
There are days when I feel like a nasty old grinch.
But Christmas is coming, I have to be good
And be careful and friendly, trying not to be rude.

Grumpy Old Bill R.

Bill Robertson

Old Men *(2011)*

Why do some old men survive?
What's the point of being alive?
They may ask themselves sometime
What it means to be sublime.

In their nineties time seems short
And most had not thought to live so long.
Where they're going next some wonder,
Most are sure they're going up yonder.

Where they think that heaven is,
Or whether there is a heavenly bliss.
Most are hopeful and do care,
With whom their journey they will share.

But what from day to day they like the most,
Is chat with guys and sometimes boast,
Of times gone bye when life was good,
And all things happened as they should.

But in the end it's all about,
Certainty not fickle doubt.
That's why as they approach the end,
Their greatest need is for a friend.

Ranipet Pantoum *(2012)*

Tired and sick they keep on coming
Hoping for the Three-day Marandu,
Doctor Sahib they seek his caring
Waiting patiently in the queue.

Hoping for the Three-day Marandu
Praying for a lucky chance
Waiting patiently in the queue
Their health they trust it will enhance.

Praying for a lucky chance
Could this be that special day
Their health they trust it will enhance
Razi palani some say.

Could this be that special day
The Marandu will cure their pain
Razi palani some say
Or will it still be all in vain?

The Marandu will cure their pain
Doctor Sahib they seek his caring
Or will it still be all in vain?
Tired and sick they keep on coming.

Poet's Comment: *'Marandu'* is the phonetic rendering of the Tamil for Medicine, pills or other medicaments taken by mouth. In our outpatient clinics at the Scudder Memorial Hospital, Ranipet, we used the term "three-day medicine", indicating that the patient was to take the medicine for three days, then return to the outpatients clinic for a further examination and if necessary a further three days supply. The clinic was free so the patients did not object to coming back after three days. The reason we doctors used this method was because the majority of our patients were uneducated villagers who were only able to count up to three days; specifically, Today, Tomorrow and The Next Day, for which there are common words in Tamil.

'Razi palana' is the phonetic rendering of the Tamil for, "What do the Stars say?" This was a common question of the villagers in regard to the diagnosis of their illness, reflecting the general belief among the people of India, in astrology. Today in the West much the same belief prevails among our general population of "ex-Christians".

Politics

The Liberals *(1970)*

The powers and joy of regal sway
Their hollowness will soon betray.

Poet's Comment: A brief outburst of disgust at the corrupt ways of the provincial Liberal politicians in Canada as I found them in the 1970s. This reaction continues over forty years later!

A Leading Liberal! *(1973)*

As rude a knave as ever grew
His manners made one want to spew.
Thy naked lust for power, beware
Of future weakness ere thou dare.
As thieves in passing loyalty bray,
Their fellows they will soon betray.

Poet's Comment: Another anti-Liberal outburst of outrage about the behavior of a leading Nova Scotia Liberal politician. It was not my last one.

To My Fellow Bureaucrats *(1979)*

The federal bureaucracy was a heaven made for you and me,
created by some fertile mind to help us through this mortal bind.

Both young and old of either sex are all alike beneath this hex,
The Francophone and Anglophone are equal and sublimely prone,
Tis not a crime ethnicity, but pure sublime duplicity.

Trudeau's Downfall *(1984)*

In the fall of '84, Pierre Elliot's reign was o'er.
A true blue knight came riding in
Free from grit and graft and sin.

He gathered in some noble knights
Skilled in tax and trade and rights.
And soon they had a glorious dream
Of how to keep their power supreme.

Provincial rights to stop Quebec,
From causing constitutional wreck.
Capital gains and tax reform
To keep Ontario from harm.

No sooner had their caucus met
They realized with deep regret
Their plans had been destroyed by PET
Who'd left them in enormous debt.

Quebec in Canada (1998)

Separate but together,
Let's stay like that forever.
From Trudeau to Martin
And Levesque to Bouchard,
They all really tried,
But found it too hard.

We needn't feel queasy
The solution is easy,
Just be happy forever
Separate but together.

Poet's Comment: There are still problems with Quebec six years after I left the federal service. It will take several generations to solve. In 2012 the situation is no better. The more that is given the more is demanded.

Pre-Presidential Election *(2012)*
A Villanelle

Romney and Obama are fighting for the crown,
No one knows exactly who is going to win,
And who will soon be king around the town.

Despite the quarrels deep in Washington,
Republicans and Democrats are really of one kin,
But Romney and Obama keep fighting for the crown.

If the 50:50 pre-vote makes you frown,
Don't worry if you think it's all a sin,
About who will soon be king around the town.

Some fear a Fiscal Cliff they'll all go down,
While others see a better time begin,
As Romney and Obama are fighting for the crown.

Some will ask just who will gain renown,
Or if all is left completely in a spin.
Romney and Obama are fighting for the crown,
And who will soon be king around the town.

Presidential Election *(2012)*
A Villanelle

Barack Obama won again,
He beat Mitt Romney fair and square.
Four more years extends his reign.

Republican politicians cannot complain,
They kept The House, it is their share.
Barack Obama won again.

The Fiscal Cliff looms quite insane,
Warning Barack he'd better take care.
Four more years extends his reign.

Canadians seem happy with Obama's gain,
Hoping his trade policies will all be fair.
Barack Obama won again.

Whatever the future holds, tis plain,
The US and Canada will be a strong pair.
Barack Obama won again,
Four more years extends his reign.

Miscellaneous

First Love *(1954)*

If I to thee my love could tell
And by some gentle magic spell
My thoughts of thee give verbal form
And heavy stumbling words transform
Then, thou sweet maiden soon would know
And with these heaven-sent phrases glow
To hear how far and wide and deep
That I of love for thee do keep
How true my love is they'd recount
How pure the stream from Cupid's fount
A love with passion warmly blended
Yet finely tempered; from lust defended
Alas! When 'neath our trysting lamp
My voice is dumb, my tongue takes cramp!
A first attempt I pray excuse
My love is true, if not my Muse!

Poet's Comment: This was my first love-sick outpouring as a young twenty-five year old, to someone who I thought was a still an innocent young woman of the very highest moral standard.

True Love *(1957)*

Love is blind men say, tis true
For so did God ordain
That man seek love with veiled sight
And knowing not its pain.

But ah! That pain when once tis found
We ne'er are blind again
And ever more we see the faults
Of all our fellow men.

Then love so soon beyond our ken
Is vain and out of reach?
Alone tis so, but God has sent
His Son the Way to teach.

The essence of that love most true
Is strength and selflessness
And purity and staying power
Those virtues God does bless.

And others weak and selfish ways
As blind if we forgive
To the extent that we love them
So we in peace shall live.

In the Woodlands *(1999)*

Garry Oaks stand in clustered embrace,
happy to spread a dappled shade o'er their age-old meadow.
Snowberry, Indian Plum and Oceanspray,
nestle thankfully around the gnarled trunks.

Mahonia, Nootka Rose and glades of Licorice Fern join in
silent gratitude, sheltering a thousand, thousand gentle plants,
each offering its own perfection, in shades of blue and pink,
red and yellow.

Some neat and small can miss the casual eye,
while beds of Easter Lily and carpets of Camus
spread their radiant charm for all to see, in the Woodlands.

A Woodland Ditty *(2001)*
(Can be sung to the tune, "If you go down in the woods today")

If you go down in the woods today
You're sure of a big surprise.
When down the path you wind your way
You won't believe your eyes!

Optional Chorus:

When the Friends were young and the Broom was high
And blackberry bushes reached to the sky
We all worked hard at pulling the Broom, in the Woodland.

In those first days we worked blistered and tired
It wasn't the easiest thing.
While Dr. Lam our spirits kept fired
We worked right through to the Spring.
Chorus:

With hearts aflame, but not seeking for fame
We fought for indigenous plants.
We lopped and cleared old plants to reclaim
As if we had ants in our pants.
Chorus:

And now at the dawn of the Millennium
We look on those long nine years.
In spring we can see lots of Erythronium,
Which vanquishes all our fears.
Chorus:

Now here and there the ground was all bare
But it hasn't lasted long.
There's no more Broom or blackberry there
And nothing indigenously wrong.
Chorus:

And when you're there, you'll see volunteers,
Who seldom stop for a rest.
If not their heads, then surely their rears,
They always do only their best.
Chorus:

In winter-time when mosses are green
Camus lies quiet in the soil,
And licorous fern is everywhere seen
While broom is just waiting to spoil.
Chorus:

We're hard-working groups of girls and of guys,
Who never give up or complain.
We work all year round to no ones surprise
And know that it's never in vain.
Chorus:

Map Dream *(2000)*

One day in a dream he did fly,
An old man on a carpet up high.
He sensed it was aimed quite specific,
As it skimmed right across the Pacific.

Soon he gazed at a land full of wonder,
And he knew he'd arrived at Down Under.
Twas the north of Australia he'd sighted,
And at Darwin's fair city alighted.

In his dream he did see a fine map,
Which his nephew had put in his lap.
So by Dangalaba and Larrakia,
He'd land at "daliladilba".

Later he visited Ngaliwurru,
Banatjarl, Katherine and Manbulloo too.
By the Coolibah route to Daguragu,
Then a swing back up north to old Jabiru.

To the east o'er the route to Urapunga,
Then away south to Alice and Mbantuarinya.
Moving on by the Ranken to Burramurra,
He got lost in the region of Billangarnah.

Back at home sitting quiet in his lazy-boy chair,
He heard drumming and humming sounds just everywhere.
It was all very strange, but he knew it was true,
He could still hear the sound of the didgeridoo!

Poet's Comment: This was encouraged by a letter from a nephew and his wife in Australia.

Deer Me

(Dictated to me by Ernest Stag. 2002!)

As I go wandering o'er the Ridge
Agrazing old ancestral trails,
Sometimes I hear despondent cries
"Dear me! Dear me!" dejected sighs.

My folks are here for many years
And know full well life's vale of tears.
Our forest home has known its woes
Through fire and storm it's suffered blows.

Some time ago, you people came
With ax and saw our home to maim.
Twas soon as bald as any coot
And no one seemed to care a hoot.

And now you have a house to live in
I trust that I may be forgiven,
The sundry swipes and tasty bites
That I enjoy on starry nights!

As you well know, there isn't much
That nightly can escape my touch!
Your list of deer-proof plants is long
But, as you know, it's mainly wrong!

Some plants do give me quite a quiver
Twixt sheer delight and fulsome shiver.
Again there's others which I eat
Only when tender, fine and sweet!

If truth be told I'm getting old
But sadly have no pension gold.
So when you see me, have a thought,
Please don't put netting on your lot!
And if temptation's evil surge
Prompts you to some deadly purge,

I counsel please, to stop and mull,
Before our herd you try to cull!
Remember we are Buck and Doe,
We have our way to plant and sow!
Our annual quadrupedic urge,
Could bear a mighty fawning splurge!

So when you sigh, "Dear me, Dear me,"
Recall this thought when you me see.
Oh Ridger, Ridger I do plead,
That you my nibbling rights concede!

Poet's Comment: The life of a deer at Arbutus Ridge, Cobble Hill, B.C.

Bill Robertson

Retrotransposon *(2003)*

A Retrotransposon am I, in chromosomal secret I lie,
Though really quite useless and oft parasitic,
Sometimes I forget that I'm truly prolific.
It's been found I protect body cells from decay,
And this since the dawn of the Dinosaur's day!

Dietary Caution *(2006)*

The cantaloupe and the cookie came riding into town,
And tho' I had not met them they soon were gobbled down.
Twas early the next morning, afore the early dawn,
A pain came on quite suddenly and left me all forlorn.
I knew it was the cookie that did the deadly deed,
Henceforth with sober caution that cookie I shall heed.

The Garden at 563 Cedar Crescent *(2008)*

Our garden in Arbutus,
Is a place we love to be.
The Rhodos in the springtime,
Are magnificent to see.

Underneath the Weeping Birch,
A flood of Daffodil,
In varied hues of yellow,
Admiring eyes they fill.

Spreading 'neath the trees and Rhodos,
Purple-blue Ajuga blooms,
With Sedum's scattered reddish hues,
And Lithodoras dainty blues.

Calluna aureofolia,
Blends its reddish hue,
With leaves of red Japonica,
And beds of Hidcote blue.

Digitalis purpura,
Stands tall in days of June,
Among the Saxifragia,
And Stachys gentle plumes.

The herb bed's tasty promise,
Of Oregano and Thyme,
Of Allium and Marjoram,
And Salvia and Balm.

Our garden is a haven
Of beauty, peace and joy,
Of sounds and scents and sights,
And things that never cloy.

And as the years go onwards,
As seasons come and go,
Our garden stands perennial,
A wondrous, endless flow.

Poet's Comment: This helps me to remember the garden God helped me to create at our home on Arbutus Ridge.

Growing Old *(2009)*

With passing years grow old with grace
Keep striving towards what ere you should
But do not fear to lose the race.

If failure you have had to face
Resist the tendency to brood
With passing years grow old with grace.

When passions joys do lose their pace
Let not depressive thoughts intrude
And do not fear to lose the race.

As memories seem hard to trace
Recall whatever ones you could
With passing years grow old with grace.

When losses threaten to debase
With strength maintain a positive mood
And do not fear to lose the race.

If Fortune should your cause deface
With courage do as you see good
With passing years grow old with grace
And do not fear to lose the race.

The Trees *(2009)*

I am grown old and watch the trees
Survivors from an ancient era
One by one their time must come.
"Darkens my yard, threatens my roof", some cry.

The trees know their time will come sooner than later,
But like silent sentinels they watch our little lives,
Our foibles and fetishes, our loves and prejudices,
Nodding or shaking their heads in wise judgment
As those who'd seen it all before we ever were.

Infinite respect is their due;
No harm I'll do as long as I am,
But one day a south-west gale may bring down
Those who lost the protection of the forest,
Or an earthquake may destroy this Ridge and take us all away;
But the thousand tree seeds will all their strength renew
And recreate the forest where it stood.
That would be good.

Ode to April *(2009)*

The North West wind blowing away the first spring blooms.
Beauty scarce-born now cast away, while bees as busy seek their nectar's gold.
A cool spring after the seven years repeated El Nino has upset
the even tenor of our north-west Pacific weather pattern.

As the economy of the United States slowly struggles
to recover from the disastrous times of financial greed,
by too many Boomer opportunists whose avaricious appetites
consumed other's resources, impoverishing not only a nation
but a world, before escaping to some island refuge and its material joys,
So we too may suffer for our petty selfish sins.

Villanelle on Same-sex Marriage *(2009)*
A satire

The latest style in sexual proximity
Is same-sex marriage the way of the gay?
When all that's desired is to couple with dignity,

And ensure the approval of Western society
While leaving its opponents in much disarray
On the latest style in sexual proximity.

But conservatives feared it would lead to iniquity
And called on the people to kneel down and pray
When all that's desired is to couple with dignity.

Some felt it could boost all kinds of variety
Making most of the people cringe in dismay
At the latest style in sexual proximity.

Could polygamy spread causing much impropriety
Or marriage to animals become a new way?
When all that's desired is to couple with dignity.

Prayers are being said to the highest divinity
In the hope that the problem will just go away
From the latest style in sexual proximity
When all that's desired is to couple with dignity.

Decision Time *(2011)*

Challenges come and choices present
Options appear of every intent.
The pros and cons must be fully assessed
Decisions are made as to what's for the best.

We're happiest thinking that things will not change
Too many choices to plan and arrange
Intuition is ours and it plays its part
Objectives are clear and we're ready to start.

Quick to the action we answer the call
Renewed energy speeds us on to our goal
With increasing certainty decisions are made
A spiritual fire has come to our aid.

Villanelle on Moving *(2011)*

Moves are good when fortune blessings bring
And life seems better than its been before
But move one must from fickle Nature's sting.

The benefits of moving often ring
And in one's heart they haply good things pour
Moves are good when fortune blessings bring.

When moving snags appear good luck takes wing
And all our well-thought plans give less not more
But move one must from fickle Nature's sting.

New challenges our praises oft-times sing
They give us hope good things will come galore
Moves are good when fortune blessings bring.

With new surrounds a warning bell may ring
To face us with some things we can't ignore
But move one must from fickle Nature's sting.

In balanced moderate moves success is king
Carrying the seeker safe to happy shore
Moves are good when fortune blessings bring
But move one must from fickle Nature's sting.

Bill Robertson

Global Destruction *(2011)*

Disaster and destruction most certainly will come,
Leaving few survivors, desperate and dumb.
Whether earthquake or tsunami,
It will hit the world a whammy.
People's bodies all entangled,
Countless millions dead and mangled.

Poet's Comment: They say our earthquake is overdue.

The End *(2011)*

Whether earthquake or tsunami
It will hit the world a whammy.
People's bodies all entangled,
Leaving millions dead and mangled.

From where foul blight could it arise?
Deep in Earth's crust, there danger lies.
Through cracks and holes Death's heralds pour,
With frightening power and thundering roar.

Such dreadful things why would they come,
We cannot guess or count their sum.
By prayer we'll hope to shield our fate,
Support us in that awful wait.

Disaster and Destruction most certainly will come,
Leaving few survivors desperate and numb!

Bill Robertson

Earth's Coming *(2012)*

God the creative non-vibration,
The universe is His creation.
Within its compass, suns and planets,
Milky Ways and countless starlets,
All solid, liquid, gaseous stuff,
With plants and animals quite enough.
Somewhere far out in a galaxy void,
He set out to create His first humanoid.

Far back in time in a bygone year,
That humanoid He made appear.
Its nearest forebear was an ape,
Genetically happy to make its escape,
From the trials and fears of a primitive life,
Trying to survive in a world full of strife.
With extraterrestrial help we progressed,
But still haven't reached all the way to our best.

In a planet outside of our own solar system,
The secret of life had arrived and was with them.
One day it was drawn into our space,
And in time was the reason that we found a place.
Its people and culture were highly advanced,
They made us a planet and left us enhanced.
To satisfy His primal plan,
They then began to make a man!

Poet's Comment: This is a first attempt at explaining how we appeared on Earth with extraterrestrial help.

175

Moving Madness or Spring Fever *(2012)*

Looking back a year has passed,
So many souls we've met and known.
Some whose goals they far surpassed,
Others just survived alone.

Residents know the cost's not cheap,
Though all the millionaires approve.
While some folks find it rather steep,
And wonder if they'll have to move.

There's Tom and Betty, Jean and Fred,
Though happy now may soon be dead.
We're all the same if it comes to that,
Some are thin and some are fat.

On Saturday the thought was changed,
Our moving plans were rearranged.
A day of searching was enough,
To prove the task was much too rough.

So now we'll just sit out and wait,
For God's good guidance on our fate.
We may now never make a move,
And just enjoy our comfy groove.

A Dying Breed *(2012)*

Within our generation strong survivors we
But most of us will surely go by twenty twenty-three
The world is moving faster with every passing year
The Boomer generation along with "X" and "Y",
Seem out of touch with what to do and where and when and why.
An underlying atmosphere is tinged with dread and fear
The standards of morality continue to go down,
And Humpty Dumpty's fallen and has a broken crown.
It seems as if the Boomers along with "X" and "Y",
Are lost and don't know what to do at all, or why.
If they don't waken up quite soon,
They'll never colonize the Moon!

If only they'd ask me what to do,
But sad to say they never do, boo-hoo, boo-hoo.

Ode to Hogmanay *(2012)*

Oh Hogmanay's a passing day
A year of life has passed away
Looking back at what it meant
And did it leave a calm content.

But as one contemplates the past
Another year is coming fast
Do not fear of getting old
Face the future brave and bold.

Some propose fine resolutions
Leading on to grand solutions.
Others fearful of the task
Veil their thoughts behind a mask.

At Berwick in the afternoon,
Relatives come both late and soon
Carrying bags as if commanded
They would not come if empty-handed.

And well before the sun has set
The young ones take their leave and let
Their elders dress up for the dinner
At Hogmanay it is a winner!

Their feast upon the dying year
Has finest food and cups of cheer
The band tunes up for old-tyme dancing
And sets the stage for fun and prancing.

Its true those in their eighties and nineties
Should be in bed and in their nighties
But two or three are still quite sprightly
And dance and jig around quite lightly.

But when on New Year's morn they rise
A few confess it was unwise
To dance and prance away the night,
And now have joints so sore and tight.

At Berwick on the Hogmanay
There's many there who like to play
But some who like to dance and jink
Had better stop and have a think!

Snifflessness *(2013)*

There was a wee doggie who had no sniffer
So she didn't know when her fridge was a whiffer

She knew a big doggie who could sniff all the wiffs
Who found them and took some gigantic sniffs.

So they had to clean the whole thing out
With many a loud and fulsome shout.

This included solid ice
Which really wasn't very nice.

It was stuck really hard and very tight
To melt it took a day and a night

But now it's clean and back to normal
And wee doggie as usual is queenly regal.

The Yugas *(2013)*

(Kali Yuga)

The Kali Yuga reached its nadir
A time of violence, hate and fear.
Mankind was struggling in the darkest age,
With little help from saint or sage.

The average man of every race,
Must needs accept a lowly place.
Enjoying some drink and sex and food,
Avoiding ills was what was good.

Even for those with power and money,
Life was not just milk and honey.
Fighting wars to keep their land,
And everything got out of hand.

It's good that Kali Yuga is past,
And better years are climbing fast.
So now we'll give a grand hurrah
To welcome rising Dwapara!

(Dwapara Yuga)

Ascending Dwapara came on strong,
Two thousand four hundred years long
Perceptive Understanding is Dwapara man's strength
Well above Kali Yuga's limited length.

His forte is Self Interest as we all know so well,
Widespread Materialism could be a warning knell.
That Selfishness would never be the wisest way to go
To make the world a better place for everyone to know.

He needs Awakened Intellect
Ascending Dwapara's key object.
Energy Awareness within an Age of Reason,
Human Rights and Happiness will give it all cohesion.

(Treta Yuga)

In four thousand one hundred Treta rolls in
The Silver Age is about to begin.
It will last three thousand wonderful years,
And take away so many fears.

As the Age ascends we'll become telepathic
Reading minds will be quite automatic.
If puzzled by any predicament,
We'll solve it by Intuitive Attunement.

In Treta Self Mastery for everyone,
Will be the key to what we've done.
We'll all be blessed with Thought Awareness,
The spoken word will be much less.

(Satya Yuga)

Around the seven thousand seven hundred year,
Treta people will know that change is near,
They'll feel that wondrous years are due,
A heaven on Earth, it will be true.

A Golden Age of virtue and purity
Egos controlled to a perfect simplicity,
We'll each have direct intuitive perception
Rejoicing with God in total absorption.

Poet's Comments: In India, the Great Year of mankind is referred to as the Maha Yuga. The Yugas refer to the different ages of mankind, identified by the Greeks as Iron Age, Bronze Age, Silver Age and Golden Age. According to the Indian sages we have entered the Dwapara Yuga, a time of positive change. The following table is provided to describe these changes.

The Yugas				
Yugas	**Called**	**Ascending**	**Descending**	**# of Years**
Kali Yuga	Iron Age	500 AD to 1700 AD	700 BC to 500 AD	2400
Dwapara Yuga	Bronze Age	1700 AD to 4100 AD	3100 BC to 700 BC	4800
Treta Yuga	Silver Age	4100 AD to 7700 AD	6700 BC to 3100 BC	7200
Satya Yuga	Golden Age	7700 AD to 12500 AD	11500 BC to 6700 BC	9600

References

Pantoum: The *'Pantoum'* is Malayan in origin and came into English language poetry through France. It is derived from the Malayan word pantun. Victor Hugo was not the first to use the form but he gave it fashion and popularity in his book 'orientales'. The pantoum works by quatrains. The quatrains are repeated and the pattern within them are required. The length of the poem is left to the poet.

Sonnet: A *'Sonnet'* is a poetic form which originated in Italy; the Sicilian poet Giacomo Da Lentini is credited with its invention. The term *sonnet* derives from the Italian word *sonetto*. By the thirteenth century it signified a poem of fourteen lines that follows a strict rhyme scheme and specific structure. One of the best-known sonnet writers is William Shakespeare, who wrote 154 of them (not including those that appear in his plays). A Shakespearean, or English, sonnet consists of fourteen lines written in iambic pentameter, a pattern in which an unstressed syllable is followed by a stressed syllable five times.

Villanelle: The *'Villanelle'* is a poem of 19 lines with 5 stanzas. Its origin is thought to be Italian and was considered a round song, something sung with repetitive words and refrains. By the time the villanelle emerges into poetic history, it does so as a French poem in the 1600s with pastoral themes. In the 1870s in England, French poetry became an object of interest and admiration. Oscar Wilde took it up in 1891.